Beloved c
I know yo
the U spot
& I hope that the food
was tasty. Enjoy your
Day

NO ENEMY WITHIN

Your Personal Guide on How to detach from *social media* and

create a *Legendary* Character in just 14 Days

Davis J. Williams

NO ENEMY WITHIN

Cover Design Created By Jeremy Salmon at WEDESIGN

www.wedesign.media

DAVIS J. WILLIAMS

No Enemy Within presents DetoxHD, the worlds first revolutionary 14-day mindset boot camp helping to you to be the BEST VERSION OF YOURSELF… **all** of the time!

This book is FOR EVERYONE. Not just for young teenagers. Everyone wants to be a legend, regardless of your age. Are you exploring your genius? Overcoming barriers? Building an empire? Need to refocus? Whatever your situation, NO ENEMY WITHIN has been written for anyone wanting to up their game

.

"The EGO is the Enemy Within. The Ego will do anything to survive, EVEN if that means taking you out of the picture"

Davis J Williams

DEDICATIONS

I would like to dedicate this book to my four children:
Makaylah, Micah, Makeda and Makai.
You all are my fuel and I do all this for you. Make sure you
strive to do better than I!
I love you!

Dad - I think about you daily. I love you, thanks for the
inspiration.

Mum - you are such a role model to me. I have been so
blessed to have you as my mother and my lighthouse.

Desmond and Diane – thanks for instilling great values and
helping me to become the amazing person I am today – I love
you like steam broccoli and sweet potatoes.

To my wife Michelle – you are my rock, my spine and the
queen on my chessboard. I am so lucky to be with you. I love
and honour you.

To all my friends, family, the Undiluted Expressionz & Love is
Just a Verb collective and **to those who came before me** – I
thank you all! Big up my R.O.A.R business partner Albert 7 –
big things a gwan! L.I.F.E (Jay) nothing but love, Ebz, Wilz,
DLS, Daz Rock, Oscar old school and new school. Special
thanks to Neeks - thanks for all the suggestions. You're a
diamond; thanks for always acknowledging me as a role
model, your gonna blow up boo!
Abby Sonko, thanks for your educated eye. Your heart is
massive.Special shout out to the students of Preston Manor
High School & Ato Carboo. Without you guys this book would
not have materialised. You guys are awesome!

"If you have BIG DREAMS you gotta have a BIG MINDSET"
Davis J Williams

DAVIS J. WILLIAMS

Table of Contents

The Introduction by Davis J Williams

"The ego, the super villain that everyone is trying to defeat"
Davis J Williams 2015

There has been a lot of talk about the ego and the effects of the ego but one thing is for sure, no one has ever seen the face of the ego; the ego is like a ghost that we blame for everything. The ego is our silent killer, the biggest villain we will ever face. This villain has special powers, this villain, called the ego can TRICK you into thinking that it is really you. Amazing huh? This villain never rests; it is with you every single day, always looking for an opening, always looking for food so it can live. For the Spider-Man fans reading this, do you remember Venom? Venom required a host, which was Peter Parker to bond with for its survival. After bonding, the symbiote (the name of the black substance in Spider-Man 2 / Marvel comics) provides its enhanced powers upon the host. When the Symbiote bonded with Peter a new being was created, and that being is known as Venom.

Let us look at Beyoncé. Beyoncé said, "I have someone else that takes over when it's time for me to work and when I'm on stage, this alter ego that I've created that kind of protects me and who I really am." By this statement, Beyoncé was talking about her onstage personality – Sasha Fierce. Here Beyoncé is admitting to having an ego who she claims is called Sasha, and Sasha has her own personality, beliefs, views etc.

I have called this book No Enemy Within because I want you, the reader to take back control over your life. YES, it is your life and if you are not careful you will let the ego, the enemy within, take your identify, your dreams and your self control right from under your eyes.
'No Enemy Within' will highlight to you that the ego is only an illusion, a mask but a very powerful one preventing you from knowing just how powerfully amazing you are.

NO ENEMY WITHIN

Let us be real, with knowledge and understanding of the existence of the ego you too can do amazing things, using it to do your most courageous biddings, but if you let the ego take control, it will have its wicked way if you.

"When there is No Enemy Within, no enemy outside can ever harm you"

At the age of 21 I realised that my ego was my enemy, the amount of trouble I got into because of it was unreal. My ego was wild, it had not been trained nor had I understood exactly what it was, furthermore I did not even know it existed – all I knew was that I made some DUMB decisions, I acted so foolish. I am 100% certain that most of the WRECKLESS decisions that I made was made NOT BY ME, but by my ego pretending to be me.

I always heard the term ego this and ego that but I never really understood it, and because I didn't understand it I could never defeat it?

I made so many mistakes, just like you. Mistakes where I refused to take any responsibility for my actions. Just like you. The bigger the mistake the larger the impact and the longer the ripples. After a while I got tired of always defending myself, always fighting to be right, frustrated with life and always waiting for someone else to put their neck on the line and make things right. I was sick and tired of being sick and tired. I decided to stop running and face up to my fears, and that was when I noticed the power of my ego.

My ego was the false idea of who I was. Imagine looking into the mirror, what you see is backwards, you see your reflection. Your left hand is your right, the words written on your tee shirt appears back to front but you understand that this is a backward view that you are seeing. You don't confuse reality with the image in the mirror do you?

Your ego (your reflection, your mask) always wants to impress others. It is so concerned with how others think, it always wants to be right, look good and protect its image, and trust me, it will do anything to maintain the image, and the act it has created.

Understanding the Enemy Within
The ego has been with us since we became aware as a child. The ego constantly receives information and translates it to suit itself, once the translation is complete; it gives you the false message. These messages are designed to PROTECT the IMAGE that the EGO has CREATED. IT IS NOT THE REAL YOU.
My ego was terrified of feeling worthless, it was impatient because it did not want to loose out on opportunities, it always compared itself to other people, it would never accept responsibility, it would blames others when things didn't go its way, it always wanted to be in control… total control, and if it wasn't in control it would sulk and press that self destruct button and mess everything up.

Not only did my ego obsessed with image and looking good, my ego also loved being comfortable. It hated change, it hated growth, it hated development and it was at this moment where I created detoxHD, the worlds only virtual mind-set detox designed to tame the ego and become legendary in character. Remember, you were born legendary, greatness is within, and you just jumped off the path temporarily, now its time to jump back on that wave.

If my ego had its own way it would keep me in the same job, the same dead end relationships, the same old arguments, the same excuses and the same problems. The ego would be happy with me going around in circles, as long as it's existence is not threatened.

Stop harming yourself with alcohol and drugs abuse, cigarettes, over eating or overspending to numb the discontentment and dissatisfaction you feel as a result of living in the illusion of a comfort zone created by your ego.

"The magic takes place outside of your comfort zone, and your ego hates it there, to explore personal growth, explore what's outside of that zone" Davis J Williams

Our detox has nothing to do with food (you will be glad to know). DetoxHD requires students to unplug from all distractions such as; social media (Facebook, Instagram, Twitter, Snapchat) television, arguments, negative music (music promoting drugs/violence) computer games, time wasting for fourteen (14) days. We want you to unplug from the external world so you can PLUG into them, you dreams, goals and you purpose. The ego will test you, but that's the whole point. You only become better as a game when you play better opponents. Unplugging from social media is the easy part and your ego might tolerate it. When we say HD we are not referring to the resolution of one's television; it involves character-building and lifestyle adjustment challenges designed to disrupt patterns of negative thinking, damaging habits, egotistical and unproductive attitudes.

1. By engaging totally with the detoxHD challenge you will gradually overcome materialism. Companies like Tesco, MC Donald's and Coco Cola target the ego with their adverts. You sometimes sit their laughing at how stupid an advert might be but remember, the advert was not for you, it was for your ego. These companies make you us believe you will feel better if you bought their product. DetoxHD increasing self-esteem through highlighting your natural abilities - your sense of humour, your drive, and your passion – and this breaks the ego's materialistic bondage.

2. DetoxHD also helps you break free from the past. Your ego does not like the unknown, and that is why it likes the comfort zone. Comfort zones contain your past memories - good or bad – which are familiar, comfortable and unchallenging. DetoxHD realise your past does not define you, nor will it dictate your future. The ego is not evil, it just wants to keep you safe - by being comfortable – and every time you live in the past you do not get to create the present and the future that you dreamt of.

3. DetoxHD challenges all inferiority complexes. "I am not good enough" is the language of the ego. You will never be good enough and any achievements will be played down. Overcome the ego by focusing on yourself and not always watching and comparing yourself to others, dance to the beat of your own drum,

4. Remember that the ego just wants you to be safe and sound. If it could it would wrap you up in bubble-wrap! Have you noticed that when things seem to be headed in a good direction, your ego anticipates that someone bad will happen real soon so to avoid pain and unhappiness the ego presses the self-destruct button. DetoxHD wants you to be brave; to live and have a phenomenal life, all you have to do is believe.

5. Be brave and honest about your past and your future. Be authentic, be real, everyone can see a fake! The ego doesn't like being naked - emotionally. The ego also does not like feeling vulnerable or weak so it will create a massive wall to protect you. Emotions are healthy and you should never bottle up how you feel. Bottling up these feelings are hard work, it's easier if you just let it go. Through our DetoxHD challenges you will be asked to use your emotion to help you soar in the sky with the eagles.

6. Think before you act, take your time when responding to situations. You ego is like an aggressive bodyguard; always ready to pounce and react to situations it sees as threatening.

Not only does the ego create massive protective walls, this ego can also build electric fences designed to protect the fake world it created. Step too close and you will get a shock. The ego sees every comment as an insult and any advice as criticism. To control this enemy within, think before responding and stop believing that the whole world is out to get you.

7. "There is something about yourself that you don't know. Something that you will deny even exists until it's too late to do anything about it. It's the only reason you get up in the morning, the only reason you suffer the shitty boss, the blood, the sweat and the tears. This is because you want people to know how good, attractive, generous, funny, wild and clever you really are. "Fear or revere (admire) me, but please think I'm special." We share an addiction. We're approval junkies. We're all in it for the slap on the back and the gold watch. The "hip, hip, hoorah." Look at the clever boy with the badge, polishing his trophy. Shine on, you crazy diamond. Cos we're just monkeys wrapped in suits, begging for the approval of others"

A Quote From A must watch film Revolver, watch it on YouTube.

I HAVE A DREAM... I HAVE A DREAM!

Before reading this book take a moment and think about your dreams. I believe that your dream was given to you for a reason. I don't believe you were given that dream so you could just think about it, day in and day out. I believe that you have that dream because you're supposed to fulfil that dream. I believe that you are supposed to wear that dream like a badge of honour; a dream that you should be proud to share and showcase, not a dream that you are embarrassed to talk about for fear of being judged by others.

I do not care how big this dream is; I don't care how scary that dream is. I don't even care if people laugh at them. I just want you to remember one thing...

You achieving that dream is POSSIBLE.
You fighting for that DREAM is absolutely necessary.

When you believe that you are powerful and that you have greatness within, you will notice a spring and skip in your step. Life just seems to have a different meaning! When you believe in your dreams and in your own potential you will notice that it doesn't matter how many times life spits in your face or how many barriers life throws in your way; you'll find yourself getting up and running towards that dream like you are The Terminator...I'LL BE BACK

Will it be hard? HELL YEAH! But no matter what, never GIVE UP! Keep on pushing and running towards your dreams. You might already be in pain, frustrated and dissatisfied with life, why not get a reward from it? Whatever you're going through, just keep in mind that the hard times are temporary; so USE them to build and develop your character. If it doesn't KILL YOU it will MAKE YOU STRONGER.

You can make it because YOU ARE THE ONE you have been waiting for. YOU are the one. No one can make your life happen for you!!! YOU ARE THE ONE!!! And why not? Why can't you be the one to change the world? And please tell that voice in your head telling you otherwise to **SHUT UP!** I can hear that hater from here! #NOENEMYWITHIN

When you know your worth you will understand the need to stretch, to grow and develop yourself in order to fulfil your mission. Imagine playing a computer game that has no mission, no end of level boss and no ability to upgrade to the next level of the game. That game doesn't exist. Every game has different levels and to pass that level you need to upgrade your game.

Your reasons for wanting to achieve this dream must be bigger than your excuses.

Do you deserve to fulfil your dreams?

If so, why? Why do you deserve to make it?

What's your reason? Standing right behind your answer is the fuel that will give you that turbo boost needed to get the job done. Achieving your goals and fulfilling your dreams IS POSSIBLE and NECESSARY! Believing that you are the one is ESSENTIAL. You must understand that you will never fly with the eagles if you insist on pecking the ground with the pigeons for crumbs and scraps. Read this book with your dreams in mind then say to yourself…IT IS POSSIBLE…IT IS NECCESARY…I AM THE ONE THAT I HAVE BEEN WAITING FOR. IF YOU ARE READY READ ON

No Enemy Within has been written for those who want to become better, that should be the whole population of this planet earth.

About No Enemy Within

Being amazing is just a state of mind, we get that, but living in a world where many have dedicated billions of pounds to keep you ordinary, we thought that it would be wise for us to share some key skills that will help you reclaim your glory.

No Enemy Within presents the world's first 14 day virtual boot camp; DetoxHD comes in two parts.

The first part of the detox is the unplugging and ridding yourself of distractions like social media and television for 14 days, so you can finally PLUG into yourself, your dreams, goals purpose.

The second part involves character building and lifestyle adjustment. Enemy Within is a system designed to disrupt patterns of negative thinking, damaging habits and unproductive behaviour.

Our method helps you to manage stress and above all, build skills that will equip you to overcome any challenges life throws your way, because they will come!

Ultimately everything we do is geared towards you being the best you can be. The biggest block preventing you from achieving greatness is that nagging voice in your head telling you that you're going to fail or that people will laugh at you.

Unfortunately you can't just wish yourself a better character; you must go through trials and tribulations in order to develop.

Diamonds start out as mere lumps of coal that had the potential to be the most precious gem in the world.

Coal must undergo extreme pressure to become a diamond, just like the need for YOU to undergo similar tests to develop an unbreakable, bulletproof character that will help you to:

- Communicate with influence and persuasion
- Showcase your power on the world stage
- Inspire others to find their inner hero
- Embrace fear (not overcome fear because fear will always be there)
- Feel in control of your life, all the time, no matter how testing things might get
- Control all of your affairs with style, passion and grace

The challenges are necessary

If nothing else moves you, life will. You have two choices, you can change on your terms or life will force you to change. The challenges contained within this book have been designed to push you towards positive change, change that will empower you to be ready for anything life throws your way.

What is the alternative? You do nothing. And when you least expect it life will show up and smash you in the face with a baseball bat. You need to make sure you're in the driving seat of your life at all times.

The Birth of the detoxHD – The 7 Day Experiment

DetoxHD is the name given to our 14-Day Mindset Boot Camp. It all began in late December 2014 when I was teaching a small group of young people aged 13 to 15 years old about preparing for the New Year, setting their necessary goals and being the best they could be. These students were known to have a bad reputation and they were on the teacher's hit list. The students file said that they were anti-social, troubled and failing behind in all areas of school; I was commissioned to help regulate their behavior and encourage them to achieve in school by enrolling them into my development programme.

One day I entered the classroom and noticed the group engaged in highly charged discussion about a recent fight and how the situation would escalate after school. I remember watching them; they were so animated and excited as they all shared their version of events, trying to predict the how it would all end. There were mentions of knives, stabbings, beat downs and all sorts, their description was so detailed. After a while I joined the group but stayed silent, allowing them to continue with their conversation.

Long before this, when I first began delivering weekly sessions, we spent an hour discussing all the things they valued in life including their goals and values.

I was impressed by their contributions, which were positive and innovative; so now, listening to this conversation I heard how distant they were from the things they valued, from their goals and aspirations; it was quite concerned, because I had thought they were making progress.

"You guys are fake, you're not real; you're a product created by Big Brother. Listen to how you lot are celebrating hurting someone that looks just like you."

After building up an amazing rapport with them over a period of weeks I could speak to them like this - rough, raw and unapologetic; they always said that they valued my 'real life' approach. I had definitely earned their respect and trust.

One of the young leaders stood up and told me that they were not slaves and they could do whatever they wanted

"Sir, seriously, we're not slaves, our behavior is by choice. We can choose to behave this way, and we can choose not to. We have the power…that is what you always told us."

They all laughed and so did I; I guess I taught them well. Still feeling frustrated by what I had heard, I set them the ultimate challenge. I knew this challenge would prove my point about them being enslaved to 'Big Brother'.

"Ok then boys I've got the ultimate challenge for you, seeing that you have the power to change. I challenge you to be great! I challenge you to be the best you can be for seven days. (That's right. The original challenge was 7 days)

As well as being great I challenge you to no computer games, no social media sites, no arguments, no fights, no TV programmes, no acting small and mediocre and no time wasting for 7 days.... I bet no one can step up."

I expected them to say they couldn't resist the temptations. I thought they'd say they couldn't control themselves therefore making me right. I expected them to admit that they were slaves to the system.

But I was wrong, they didn't.

Instead, to my surprise, every single one of these young men stepped up to the challenge. Not only did they take it on, they destroyed it and gave it new meaning. They refused to let me win.

For seven days they excelled in their subjects, they mastered their situations, they were positive, influential, impactful and above all, happy. Their levels of focus and personal growth increased and for seven days, they were phenomenal.

Everything that these students did throughout the 7-day challenge has been documented in this book.

Since then DetoxHD has developed into a 14–day mindset boot camp designed to take people out of your comfort zone, have some fun and live their life to the fullest.

The core principles of DetoxHD are based on those given to my pupils who took the very first detox.

It is funny how the most amazing things can happen out of impulse. DetoxHD wasn't intentional, it was a dare created from nothing, and it was only mentioned because I wanted to win a debate with some students, now look at what happened…There are opportunities in every encounter, and for once my eyes were opened and I saw the opportunity.

Is this going to be hard?

This journey can be whatever you want it to be.

If you want it to be easy, it will be, if you think it will be hard it will be. Choose wisely. Do you want to be successful? Do you want to make better choices? Do you want to be in control of your life? Do you want to be respected and get what you want? Do you want your character to be magnetic, amazingly phenomenal and invincible? Are you focusing on what you can achieve or are you focusing on how hard it will be? Where your attention goes, the energy will F.L.O.W

So my friend, don't you think it's time that you removed that **Enemy** hiding **within?** Don't you think it's time to take your life by the horns? I think it's time that you realise your full potential and leave an amazing legacy for those who will come after you - i.e. your children, family and loved ones.

No Enemy Within will definitely help destroy your bad habits, embrace those fears and bring you face to face with a brand new, amazing, head-turning you.

How to use this book

This clever little book has been written in such a way that you don't need to read the whole book in one go. Don't let its size deceive you.

It's your birthday and you are presented with a cake. Or it could be Christmas and your Mum or Dad presents you with a feast of kings containing every single one of your favourite dishes. YOU DON'T just open your mouth and scoop all the food off your plate and into your mouth do you? Nor do you run away because of the size of the feast! If you are like me you would slowly and precisely eat your meal ONE BITE at a time.

Treat this book like that meal. Take your time. Read and complete just one essay per day

"I hated every minute of training, but I said to myself, "Don't quit. Suffer now and live the rest of your life as a champion."
~Muhammad Ali

Along the road to success you have to be willing to make sacrifices and do things that make you uncomfortable.

What about failure?

In 2012 a few researchers from New York University filmed more than 130 infants aged between 12 and 19 months as they explored a specially designed playroom; a further fifteen infants were filmed at home.

Some of these babies were 'expert crawlers' who had yet to start walking. Some had just taken their first steps and a few had been walking for a few months. Frame-by-frame, video analysis showed those who walked clocked up an average of 2,368 steps an hour and covered 0.44 miles; amazingly, the same infants fell down on average 17 times an hour, but those who were classified as the 'new walkers' had the most tumbles, with one unlucky child racking up 69 falls an hour. Guess what happened to those children who fell down continuously? They got up and kept on trying.

They tried and tried, they never screamed out "I CAN'T DO THIS!" they didn't quit, they never complained, they just kept on trying.

What is failure? Failure is not always a mistake, or that you yourself are a failure. It may simply be the best one can do under the circumstances. The real failure is to stop trying. Failure serves a purpose. If you have failed 10,000 times, you have discovered 10,000 ways that won't work.

Michael Jordan, the world's greatest basketball player said:

"I've missed more than 9000 shots in my career. I've lost almost 300 games. Twenty-six times I've been trusted to take the game winning shot and missed. I've failed over and over and over again in my life. And that is why I succeed"

"When there is no enemy within, the
enemies outside cannot hurt you"
Ancient Saying

If you fail within the first hour of this DetoxHD challenge, it isn't the end of the world; make a note of what didn't work and try again, again, again and again.

The Rules

For fourteen (14) days there will be:

NO SOCIAL MEDIA (total black-out)
NO Snapchat, Instagram, Facebook, Twitter etc.
NO TELEVISION at all
NO NEGATIVE BEHAVIOUR
NO FIGHTING or ARGUMENTS
NO Candy Crush or other TIME WASTING GAMES
NO GAMING **i.e. NO** PS4 / **NO** XBOX
NO Gangster Rap / Trap / Music that promotes drugs, violence or disrespect towards members of the opposite sex

YES to YouTube for research purposes or watching MOTIVATIONAL VIDEOS **ONLY**!
YES to Text Messages (**Only** positive interactions)
YES to Socializing. You can still hang out with your friends providing they are being positive!
YES to being in TOTAL control of your MIND
YES to being totally amazing for 14 days
Yes to failure. If it goes wrong…KEEP GOING!
YES TO WAKING UP EARLY so I CAN MAXIMISE my day

I (print your name) Charlotte Cral **promise to complete all tasks to the best of my ability and I promise not to quit like I have done in the past.**

Make this promise to yourself!

Sign _Mine_ **Date** 1/06/18

Failure to plan is a plan for failure

Before you begin the DetoxHD there are a few things you need to do to first to prepare yourself.

STEP 1: COMPLETE THE STARTER ACTIVITIES LISTED AS These starter activities are designed to help prepare you for what's to come and also introduce you to the things you really want.

Starter Activity 1 - Identify your values?

Starter Activity 2 - What are your goals?

Starter Activity 2a - What do you want to achieve?

Starter Activity 3 - Identify your support

Starter Activity 4 - Identify who you want to be

STEP 2: Each day read the inspirational story (one story per day) and complete the daily challenge. End each day by completing the journal.

STEP 3: Notice the shift in your mindset and how powerful you feel. Embrace that feeling. You might get scared of the power that you will possess, that's normal, don't worry though, that fear will pass!

"When I told my mum I was doing a social media detox she laughed telling me I wouldn't be able to do it. So I went to my bedroom, removed my TV and began. I am so glad that I did the challenge because I have grown so much. I now have a clear vision of where I want to be in life."

DetoxHD participant, 13 years old

MIND out of my way

By Davis J Williams

I just got on the bus…Entry in my phone!
I just had an argument… Entry on Facebook!
About to go to bed… Updated Twitter!
I am bored and lonely… Sent a Snap Chat to my friends!
I just sneezed… Took a picture of my snotty tissues and posted it on Instagram!
That was an awkward moment… Whats App…Where are you at?

What kind of world are we now living in? Many of us have probably been here; where we literally feel compelled to post about every aspect of our day. If you're not sure what I mean, all is will soon be made clear. I'm talking about the social media takeover.

People updating their Facebook or Twitter feeds every second of the day has become common, with one study suggesting that social media is more addictive than alcohol and cigarettes. Although I appreciate there are many positive uses of social media: connecting, networking, reading news and obtaining information I am here to talk about the flip side of social media, the flip side that has taken the scalp of billions

I am sitting on the Overground Train going to work, and every person is glued to his or her mobile phone.

This is a regular occurrence that I find the most concerning is not the number of adults who are 'hooked' by their phones and countless social media apps, but the ever increasing number of teenagers being over-stimulated by Facebook, Snap Chat, Whats App or Instagram. It's said that social media addiction can lead to anxiety and stress and can damage relationships, even threaten the family unit.

I remember when Chris Brown and Rihanna had their domestic violence incident like it was yesterday. I jumped on Facebook that morning and on seeing the news engaged in the inevitable online banter, the sharing of funny images, and most importantly engaging in the numerous debates about domestic violence. Was his behaviour justified? By lunchtime I had my phone charging on my laptop and continued the social marathon until 11pm that night. 11pm. The entire day spent watching, engaging and making a mockery of these celebrities.

I was so engrossed in the jokes, the mockery, ridicule, the debates and the connections with friends and strangers alike that before I had realized, I was bouncing between Facebook, Instagram and WhatsApp for 13 hours straight.

13 hours on social media. ARE YOU KIDDING ME?

I was so involved I forgot to eat, I didn't fulfill my goals for the day, and I missed two meetings and even missed a deadline. It was crazy. Social media had actually sucked up my day.

It did not end there!

Prior to the social media boom my phone used to ring constantly and my friends and I would engage in wholesome conversations. But slowly I noticed that the phone calls reduced, whilst the "**ping**, **ping**, **ping**, **ping**, **ping**" notifications would increase.

Before I knew it I found myself messaging people instead of calling them. I remember once when phone did not ping for one whole hour, I was convinced my handset had broken.

My phone and I had become one!

What is at stake?

The mind is your most prized possession. The owners of Facebook, Sony and Apple know this. Why do you think they invest BILLIONS of pounds on advertising?

They want your mind, they want your attention. PAY attention now has a new meaning.

As the saying goes, *'Where attention goes, energy flows'*. *If you don't take the time to pay attention to the things that matter to you, then you're only enriching and nourishing someone else's dream with the attention you willingly give to them.*

Your mind is like a garden and the things you think about are the seeds. You can grow flowers or you can grow weeds. I knew for sure, my garden was full of weeds, and I don't blame Facebook, the popular free social networking website that allows you to create profiles, upload photos and videos, send messages and keep in touch with friends, family and colleagues. I BLAME MYSELF for allowing it to happen.

I helped Facebook become a billion dollar company, and in return Facebook gave me bags under my eyes.

The mind is a funny thing because on the one hand it can serve us well, make us money and bring us great joy and amazement. But if mistreated or manipulated by others, it can bring hell, fire and destruction to our doorsteps.

Having said all that, I am inviting you, dear reader, to take on this 14-Day DetoxHD challenge because I truly believe that we are **all** in need of a new mindset.

Detox: a process or period of time in which one abstains from or rids the body of toxic or unhealthy substances; detoxification

HD: High Definition; amazing quality **DetoxHD:** A detox that transforms an average person into an extraordinary being!

It took me just two evenings to truly understand the power of my mind. Before, I would waste those two evenings on Grand Theft Auto, Empire or Facebook, but instead I dedicated that time to the DetoxHD. The return I got was LIFE CHANGING.

What I am about to share with you really did BLOW MY MIND. Seriously, when I read this, I understood why so many social media networks and other major companies like Coco Cola, McDonald's and PlayStation sought my attention, mind and energy.

They had done their research.

How can I have the most prized asset on planet earth, the most complex 'thing' in human existence, but know nothing about it?

How can I have a tool that can bring me billions but not know anything about it?

These billion dollar companies understand that the miracle working power of your mind can bring you riches or make you broke, can make you sick or heal you from cancer, can make you happy and joyous or give you a life full of hell.

Your mind is your greatest gift and knowing this is your first step to greatness.

The first two evenings of my DetoxHD I decided to dedicate my evenings to learning as much as I possibly could about the mind, its powers and to develop an understanding of why so many people with wealth (Walt Disney, Hollywood etc.) wanted it. Our minds are amazing super computers, programmed to serve us. Your mind is so powerful that it actually speaks things into existence.

These corporations know this and they spend billions to try and distract you from the fact that:

1) **The *mind is powerful beyond measure* —** *it controls all processes of the body.*

2) **The mind is always awake and alert.** When your body falls asleep in front of the TV watching Songs of Praise or The Only Way is Essex your mind hears every single thing that is being said. These programmes (programme) leave powerful suggestions in your mind and these suggestions develop into actual beliefs. As a child you were immune to them until you grew and began to understand and communicate.

As a child you could do anything, you could climb walls, turn invisible, you believed that you were the one, until you were exposed to assertions from others like:

- You can't

- You will never do that

- You will fail so there is no point trying

- The world is not perfect

- Money is the root of all evil

- It's too hard/ it's impossible/ it cannot be done

It's time to reject these words, which do nothing but instill doubt and reacquaint yourself with your inner child, that little genius.

As a child you couldn't stop those who forced these words into your mind, but now you're grown, you have a conscious choice.

3) The mind has no verbal language, it doesn't speak but it communicates via pictures and images.

My mind doesn't forget anything. I can remember my 5th birthday party, my first kiss and my first fight with much clarity and emotion.

I can see the images in my head even now just by typing the words on the screen. I am emotional about it too, despite the fact that it was many years ago.

4) **The mind cannot tell the difference between good or evil, yes or no, positive or negative.** The mind uses images to create reality. Imagine what 'I will not eat toast' looks like! The mind would have to first 'see' the toast before maybe superimposing a red cross on top of it telling me not to eat it.

Or try to **not** think of a pink elephant. Go on... try your hardest... **Don't think** of a massive pink elephant.

The mind does not process 'NOT'! So be careful what you expose your mind to.

5) **The mind takes everything literally.** Whatever I choose to watch on TV, imagine, dream or visualize, is real to my mind. My mind doesn't know the difference between reality and imagination.

You could be sleeping and dreaming about Candice, that beautiful woman from the beach you saw last week. In this dream you wined and dined her before taking her back home to get familiar. Although it was a dream your mind told your body it was real, your hormones raced as your body began to react.

Two minutes later you wake up to a wet patch in your bed — you had a wet dream. Even though it was a dream, your mind thought it was real.

6) **The mind is not bound by time.** The mind only knows NOW. Tomorrow doesn't exist because when it does it becomes today. When thinking about the future, your mind is already there; your body just needs to catch up. I know many people feel trapped in the past, traumatised and unable to move forward — the mind can be cruel or compassionate. Your mind is truly able to time travel.

Take back control of your mind...

I did not want them to have it anymore! I wanted my mind back. I wasted so much time focusing on everyone else that I forgot about myself and my own wants and needs.

I was so concerned about getting next month's pay cheque and in making my boss more money that I forgot about the wealth I had promised myself when I was younger, more rebellious and courageous.

Did I want to let someone else control my life, and the life of my children? Did I want someone to tell me that I am worth £40 per hour?

Is that how much I am worth, £40? When I was a teenager I remember having visions of being behind the wheel of a BMW, having a house in Dominica, one in Italy and another in London. I remember having big dreams. But then I started being like everyone else around me. I started being ordinary.

A different type of DETOX. A different kind of boot camp.

It doesn't matter where you are these days, you will hear the TV or radio mention the word 'detox', especially by celebrities who have jumped on the detox bandwagon. It is known that the Hollywood actor, Megan Fox regularly takes shots of apple cider vinegar as a form of detox and I heard that Beyoncé lost weight for her movie *Dreamgirls* on the lemonade or Maple Syrup diet.

A good friend of mine once ate watermelons for 14 days to rid his body of toxins. Detoxes have been around for centuries with the main aim of purifying the body. More recently these detoxes have evolved into habit-breaking challenges, which come in the form of 7, 14 or 28 day challenges. In London, England there are multi-million pound campaigns such as **Stoptober** which is a 28-day challenge to stop smoking for most of the month of October. It's based on the belief that after 28 days without a cigarette, smokers are five times more likely to give up smoking for good. There's another campaign called **Sober October** where participants abstain from drinking alcohol for a month. There's also the 7 or 28-day juice detox where people are encouraged to fight disease and eliminate toxins by drinking healthy juices and smoothies for a set time period. There are all different types of detoxes and challenges now which includes the drink water for 14 days challenge, the 30-

day press up challenge, the 7-day total silence challenge or the popular 28 day 'SQUAT' challenge where people perform squats every day for 28 days in the hopes of creating a new habit...and a firmer, better looking booty.

If these challenges work for you then great, but I have noticed that many people around me who successfully complete these challenges – and I salute them big time and respect them for their effort - after a few weeks, sometimes even days later, they revert back to the same behaviour they practiced before their particular challenge.

I have always been interested in the detox challenges because I've always known that for me to become the best version of myself, I'd have to transform my behavior. But I have been reluctant because my loved ones never seemed to transform themselves as a result of their detoxes so I never tried it, as I really didn't see the point. Things always remained the same for them afterwards.

So everything I saw told me detoxes didn't work, until a good friend introduced me to a person named Earl Nightingale.

In his 'The Strangest Secret' (search for it on YouTube) Nightingale explains that **"You become what you think about; life's greatest secret is that you become what you think about."**

Other greats also agreed with this concept.

"The mind is everything. What you think you become."

Buddha

"We become what we think about...all day long."

Ralph Waldo Emerson

"Whether you think you can or can't, you're right."

Henry Ford

"Your mind is a garden, your thoughts are the seeds, you can grow flowers or you can grow weeds"

Aset

I noticed that a lot of the challenges people around me were experiencing were based on them participating in a physical activity; however there was never a challenge or activity that focused on their MINDSET. The MIND is the SEAT of all activity so surely in order to change one's behaviour THE MINDSET MUST BE TRANSFORMED FIRST?

MINDSET is described as a fixed mental attitude that influences a person's reaction.

Welcome to DetoxHD

Preparation

Now you are committed to taking on this unique challenge, you need to prepare. Imagine going on a road trip without a map or sat nav. Imagine going on a road trip or a party without an address and your iPhone's battery has died, so you can't call anyone for directions.

Having no idea of where you are going to absolutely crazy. Who does that? Who leaves their house without knowing their final destination? Before starting your journey you need to know where you are going.

Before you begin with the DetoxHD ask yourself questions like: What kind of things do I want to achieve?

How do I want to benefit from this experience?

What changes would I like to see in my life?

What do I really value in life?

Once you prepare a clear vision for yourself and your destination, you are on your journey to success.

Understanding Values

1) Values are directions we keep moving in. Goals are what we want to achieve along the way

2) Values are leading principles that can guide us and motivate us as we move through life.

3) Goals can be achieved or 'crossed off'. Values are an ongoing process. For example, if you want to be a loving, caring, supportive partner, that is a value — an ongoing process.
If you stop being loving, caring and supportive, then you are no longer a loving, caring, supportive partner; you are no longer living by that value.

There may be certain areas that you don't value much; you may skip them if you wish.
There may be areas that overlap, for example, if you value hiking in the mountains, which may come under both physical health and recreation. It is also important that you write down what you would value if there were nothing in your way.

What's important? What do you care about? And what you would like to work towards?

When I asked the first DetoxHD participants this question this is what they said

"I value my family and would like to improve my **family** relations."

"I value my **freedom.**"

"Right now, I really value my **health** because it is not the best right now."

"I value my **RELATIONSHIP** with my man, he is all I have."

"I value my **children**, they really annoy me but my love for them is unconditional."

"I value the **brothers**, my homies, and the boys. They are my crew and I am always there for them...and they are there for me."

"I value my **education**. I am doing my G.C.S.E exams and I need to get the best grades possible otherwise I will feel like a failure."

"I value my **work**, my **career**, I love what I do."

"I value my **personal** growth."

"I value my peace of mind, my **spiritual** state is very important to me."

"I value justice in the **community**, see our people unite and grow."

"I value my **health** and well-being."

Use these examples to HELP YOU with ACTIVITY 1

Please note:

Going to the gym is not a good example of a value because what you really value is HEALTH or WELL-BEING and the GYM is the ACTIVITY used to fulfill that, not the value it. **Values are NOT activities. Values are principles**

Everything you do should complement and benefit your values.

At your own pace work through the activities and use any images to encourage you along the way.

AND TAKE YOUR TIME, IMAGINE BAKING A CAKE, YOU CANNOT SPEED UP THE BAKING PROCESS

MAKE SURE YOU TO THESE PREPARATIVE EXERCISES, THIS IS YOUR LIFE WE ARE DEALING WITH!

SET YOUR ALARM CLOCK and DEDICATE At least 45 minutes to 1 hours on the tasks mentioned in this book

Starter Exercise 1
Identifying your values

Finish the sentence Below	Write a few words about what you value (below)
Example I VALUE... MY EDUCATION	***Example*** I value my education, when I say education I am not talking about School or University, I am talking about education about life
I VALUE...	My family for being loving & true to self
I VALUE...	my health & wellbeing
I VALUE...	my expanding knowledge & seeth spiritual journey
I VALUE...	all the likeminded people entering my life

GOALS are just DREAMS with deadlines

© Newcastle Utd via Getty Images

Without goals, you have absolutely no path, let alone a destination to get to. Without goals you will most likely fail to accomplish anything. With goals, your life has **direction**, **purpose**, and **meaning**.

Set goals to conquer your needs and wants and you will get your desired results. Remember, having no goals is like running a race that has no finish line.

Starter Exercise 2 / Exploring your Goal

Types of Goals	Write a few words about your different types of goals
SOME DAY GOALS One day you will do what? (Think BIG!)	A health & wellbeing clinic
FIVE YEAR GOALS (Within the next 5 years you will have achieved what?	International well paid & booked speaker
ONE YEAR GOALS	The ability card in progress
NEXT MONTH GOALS	Got good content for the truth series
NEXT WEEKS GOALS	Built another course/workshop
TOMORROWS GOALS	Outline for course/ws
TODAY I WILL...	Be in control of ego

Starter Exercise 2a
(What do you want to achieve by completing this DetoxHD?

We'll challenge you to step out of your comfort zone and

get what you want in life

DetoxHD Goals	Write a few words about your different types of goals
GOAL 1	Stop comparing myself to others
GOAL 2	live fully in my truth
GOAL 3	Show more love

SURROUND YOURSELF WITH

THOSE ON THE SAME
MISSION AS YOU

"ASK for help...NOT because you are weak but because you want to **remain STRONG**."

Starter Exercise 3
The Inner Circle

This DetoxHD will not be successful if you decide to DO IT ALONE.

<u>Find someone to do it with,</u> encourage your close friends, work colleagues and neighbours; be prepared to step outside your comfort zone. **TELL** people around you what you are doing so they can support you. **DON'T** be ashamed; be proud that you are standing up to your ego.

Be proud knowing that you are prepared to stand up and say NO! No to being yet another statistic. No to being comfortable with a mediocre lifestyle.

For this exercise you need to name **3** people who will be in your corner during the 14-day boot camp.

CONTACT 1 **OF THE 3 names anytime you're feeling stressed, under pressure or tempted.**

Their job is to encourage, empower and help you through this magnificent journey.

DAVIS J. WILLIAMS

Name of Support	Write a few words about this person

Use these people to ensure you don't give up

Most people give up because they:
1. Expect fast results
2. Stop believing in themselves
3. Get stuck in the past
4. Fear the future and the unknown
5. Resist change
6. Give their power up
7. Feel the world owes them something
8. Never visualise what is possible
9. See failure as a sign to give up
10. Overworked and knackered
11. Fear failure more than they desire success
12. They doubt themselves by talking down on themselves
13. Dwell on their mistakes instead of the solutions

DON'T LET THIS HAPPEN TO YOU

Become the Best Version of Yourself

Starter Exercise 4 / Free Upgrade

DAVIS J. WILLIAMS

Who do you want to be?

Who are you going to be during this DetoxHD? Are you going to be confident, assertive leader or are you going to be a weak crowd-following loser? Are you going to be the same old person, the person who never really got you what you wanted or are you going to explore another aspect of your character? Some people only upgrade their mobile phone or their car; we are challenging you to upgrade **YOURSELF!**

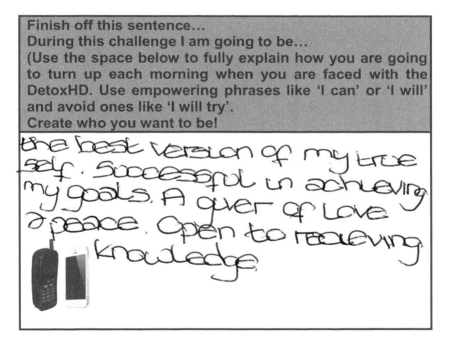

Finish off this sentence...
During this challenge I am going to be...
(Use the space below to fully explain how you are going to turn up each morning when you are faced with the DetoxHD. Use empowering phrases like 'I can' or 'I will' and avoid ones like 'I will try'.
Create who you want to be!

the best version of my true self. Successful in achieving my goals. A giver of love & peace, Open to recieving knowledge.

YOU ARE NOW READY TO BEGIN!

Reminder***
Take a deep breath & prepare to unplug from:

1) Facebook, Instagram, Twitter, Snap Chat, WhatsApp and all forms of SOCIAL MEDIA
2) Television
3) NEGATIVE MUSIC THAT PROMOTES SEX, DRUGS & MURDER
4) TELEVISION
5) ARGUMENTS
6) FIGHTING
7) COMPUTER GAMES (including those on your mobile phone or tablet)

14 DAYS OF BEING INCREDIBLE / 14 DAYS OF CONTROLLING YOUR EGO / 14 DAYS OF NO TIME WASTING

USEFUL TIPS:

Read ONE inspirational STORY per day

Complete the challenge set to the best of your ability (which can be found after the inspirational story)

Complete your journal entry each day as this helps you to monitor your progress.

WELCOME TO **DAY ONE**

"ONE DAY
YOU WILL WAKE UP
AND THERE WON'T BE
ANY MORE TIME
TO DO THE THINGS
YOU'VE ALWAYS WANTED.
DO IT NOW."

- Paulo Coelho

"It isn't the hills or mountains ahead to climb that wear you out; it is the little pebble in your shoe. Stop stressing and worrying about the little things in life, it wastes time."

Unknown

Perception

By Davis J. Williams

When I first started my DetoxHD, I struggled with self-doubt, even before I had started. I didn't believe that I could do it because at the time I was ridiculously addicted to Facebook and having conversations with all of my virtual friends who lived on it.

Upon waking up, instead of hugging my loved ones I would check to see how many likes I had received from the picture I posted the night before.

So the thought of undertaking a 14-day mindset boot camp was amazingly daunting, but I knew I had to do it.

This challenge was issued by a good friend, my mentor, so I called him to share my concerns and to investigate any loop holes that I could take advantage of.

His phone rings.

No one answers so I leave a voice message:

"Hey bro, you never answer your phone boy, but anyway,

listen...this 14 day mindset boot camp you issued me is LONG!
Come on, 14 days, are you for real? Call me back family."
I clearly struck a nerve because 5 hours later I received a
barrage of voice notes in reply to my inquiry.

Voice note One

"Davis, it is so important that you realise that time is an illusion,
there are no 14 days because time is not real, and it is a
figment of your imagination. The PAST is HISTORY...it
happened, and you can't do anything about it. The FUTURE is
a MYSTERY...that also has not happened yet so don't stress
about that which you cannot control. NOW is the GIFT that is
why it is called the present. EMBRACE now, embrace the
moment, and keep on embracing the moment. STOP worrying
about things that haven't happened yet.

Davis, pay attention...don't worry about what has not
happened, FEAR is False Evidence Appearing Real. Your
mind is playing tricks on you. Warriors don't worry; they GRIND
regardless of the season.

Davis, it's time to STOP making childish excuses, you have to
stop giving up, you have to stop wasting time and you definitely
have to stop talking down to yourself. STOP depriving yourself
of the opportunities life presents to you just because of
something that happened ten years ago."

Voice note two

"We all have our back-story; we all have a sob story of what happened when we were a child.

We are all feeling immense pain, but for some, the pain brings rewards. Don't suffer for the sake of suffering; get a reward out of it. Let the pain fuel your passion. It's time to fight back. Life is just a game and you need to play to win. You have so many options available to you. You can choose to keep on doing what your use to OR you can get up and fight. There is one thing that I can guarantee though is that the issues you face, the pain, the barriers and the huge obstacles you always talk about are not going away unless you make them go away. How many times have you tried to run away from them? How many times have you tried to ignore that obstacle by pretending that it does not exist? How many times have you tried to smoke your troubles away or by living some high speed life with the hopes of 'it' disappearing? But guess what? The obstacles didn't go away. Until you stand up and confront then, they will never go away."

Voice note three

"This challenge might be your toughest challenge yet, this challenge has your back against the wall, all your options have been exhausted, and the only thing left for you to do is for you to fight. You are a born winner. You were born to survive so embrace the moment and fight for what you believe in. This is day one of your DETOX! Treat every day like day one"

"Embrace every moment as if it was you last moment because tomorrow is not promised. Look around you...people are dropping like flies"

Voice note Four

"This is day one, promise yourself to make the decision to FIGHT for what you really want. It was you that defeated 7 billion sperm to fertilise that egg in your mother's womb, you were born to fight. It was you that fell down on average 17 times per minute when you were a baby learning how to walk.

You didn't give up; you kept on going, regardless of how many times you fell over. You have a purpose and it's time to embrace that purpose at all costs"

"Davis, whatever you are going through, trust me when I say that you can succeed. You can beat it. You are unstoppable. Insanity is doing the same thing repeatedly and expecting different results. I DARE YOU to try something different. I DARE you to stand up and fight for what you believe in. You can beat it... YOU WILL BEAT IT"

Voice note Five

"You got me fired up now boy...
Listen D, it is time to release that warrior.

(He then released a loud **LION's "ROOOAOOOR!!"** down the phone)

"Stop holding back, stop being nice and pleasant. Stop tip-toeing around your troubles; run up to your troubles and kick them down and when they are down kick them some more, give them an elbow drop and whilst doing that and let your troubles know that you are not running away any more. You are going to acknowledge your troubles, you are going to address them and you shall be victorious over them.

For years a dark force has controlled your mind and had you thinking like a sheep when in reality you are a lion. Stop being mediocre when you are supposed to be phenomenal."

Voice note ENDS

After listening several times to the messages I decided to commit 14 days of my life to doing the 14-day mindset boot camp to the best of my ability.

During those 14 days I completed this book!

"Let your dreams be bigger than your fears, let your actions be louder than your words."

EXAMPLE PROMISE LETTER

(This is an example letter. Write your own on the following page)

To my future self,

I am aware that it is my responsibly to create meaning in my life. Because I am aware I will now, from this day forward, take full responsibility for all my actions. I am the KING on the chessboard of life and I will not let anyone defeat me. I am now 100% ready to unleash my passion on the world.

To my future self, since I have met you I have been so happy.

I do not know why I was hanging out with the OLD ME, he was ok, we had some great stories but I now know that I cannot continue my journey with him because he cannot address my needs. The old me was happy sitting at the back playing small and insignificant.

NO MORE!

I am great, I am magnificent and I am important and it's necessary that I take this giant step! Everything I need to be successful is already inside me so I don't need to wait for permission from anyone. I stand before you to declare that I am here to grow and develop. I am committed to myself and the things I value the most. I will keep it moving with integrity and honour. I will not follow those on another wave. I will not worry about things that have not happened yet. I am the creator and I will succeed. OLD YOU, thank you for everything, it's time we went our separate ways. To the new me, I promise to embrace all that you offer.**No more excuses, No quitting. This is a promise to myself. It's time to make my dreams come true, I will document my dreams and turn them into a plan, into a blueprint of success, and I will follow this plan and execute it 100%.**

DAVIS J. WILLIAMS

DAY 1 TASK

PROMISE LETTER – Make Yourself a Promise

To my future self I am so excited for what is to come. I am open and ready to receive anything that will help me move forward. Positively I can feel the greatness approaching & I am 100% ready to share my true self and passion with the world.

I appreciate the old me because that version taught me some valuable life lessons BUT

I'm evolving everyday and I absolutely love who I'm becoming!!

JOURNAL ENTRY

HOW WAS DAY 1?

Describe your day. What do you need to improve on? What went well? What did you learn? Write down as much as possible!

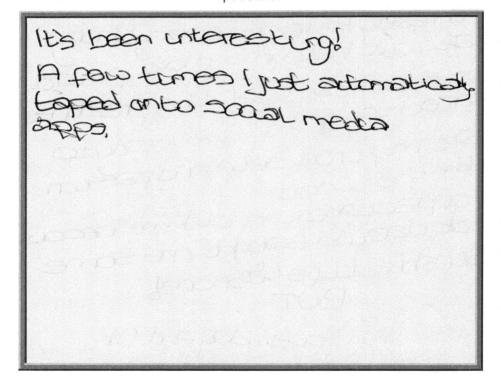

It's been interesting!
A few times I just automatically taped onto social media apps.

　　　　DAVIS J. WILLIAMS

WELCOME TO **DAY TWO**

"I am the greatest; I said that even before I knew I was."
Muhammad Ali
(Whatever you wish to become in this world, you have to act and feel like you're already that person. Use powerful statements to boost his inner ambitions)

FINDING THE LION WITHIN
By The Investigator (Andrew Muhammad)

Let me start off by giving you one of the greatest lessons I have ever learnt. This lesson can be summed up in the ten magical two letter words:

IF IT **IS** TO **BE** IT **IS** UP **TO** ME.

Life is simply what you make it. I learned in my life that if I wanted to be free it would be up to ME. How many of us spend our lives looking outwards, scanning the horizon for some mystical leader or book that will take us to heaven? Or we find ourselves believing the lie that we are not worthy of true happiness and success. Well, let me tell you this: it's time to wake up like Neo The Matrix and take the RED PILL.

You are magical, you are the best, and you are awesome. Do me a favour, stop reading, look into the mirror and tell your reflection that YOU ARE AWESOME! Do that five times a day and watch and see the difference in your life. Surround yourself with greatness and sooner or later that greatness will begin to rub off on to you.

What's the point of being a lion if you're not aware you are one?

We must become aware of our inner beauty, inner strength and royal self-esteem.

Many of you reading this may know that I am contracted to work in schools all over the United Kingdom. The objective is to motivate pupils to achieve high grades in their exams, yet I know and appreciate that in order to achieve high grades in LIFE, exam results are only a fraction of what's needed.

My life and my results transformed, based on my own level of self-awareness. In fact let me go further and say that all of our results are an expression of our own level of awareness.

The reason why I failed my school exams was that I wasn't aware that I could excel academically. The reason why I worked in jobs that I literally hated was because I wasn't aware that I did not have to tolerate that crap every day. The reason why many of us are doing what we are doing is that we are not aware that we have options.

I love to share with the youth that they are the captains of their own destiny. They control their life results; it's not with someone else or something else. So to repeat, my life transformed based on my own level of self-awareness.

That's why true education is vital. My true education started not in school but through my brother sharing his books of self-knowledge with me.

These books did more than just teach me about distant empires, dynasties and historical dates.

They broadened my awareness of the realms of possibilities.
They showed me that there were common laws of success, whether they are for individuals or nations. I also learned that this current generation of young people is probably the BEST generation we have given birth to. I look at these young warriors and I see true lions. Lions that are fearless and ready for action. There is nothing wrong with these youth.

They know this world is not right and is full of hypocrisy. At school they are rightly told not to bully others smaller than themselves and that love is the answer.

They are rightly taught that revenge solves nothing in the long run. They are also rightly taught that they should respect and honour their fellow peers. Yet when watch TV and read the newspapers they see our governments and stewards over our society do exactly the opposite. They see bigger and stronger nations bully and attack weaker and less fortunate ones for their oil and mineral wealth.
They see multinational conglomerates lining their pockets with wealth whilst the people are starving. They see international bankers crash the economic system but yet still receive multi

million pound bonuses whilst the everyday man and woman lose their jobs and livelihoods.

The youth are lions that are not aware that they are lions. My advice to the youth is to grow every day in self-awareness. Make everyday a duty to explore your values and test yourself.

Try to do something new at least once a week.

Brothers and sisters, I want my life to represent an IDEAL or a CONCEPT. I want to know that when people see my works, or me, they have the idea that nothing is impossible. They can go and achieve goals, ambitions and aspirations.
Never be afraid to be a dreamer. All successful men and women are big dreamers. They imagine what their future could be, ideal in every respect, and then they work every day toward their distant vision, that goal or purpose

Never be afraid to be financially rich. It is truly slavery teachings to believe richness is equated to being evil and poorness equates to righteousness. Some of the best friends I have are financially rich and they are like saints.

By contrast some of the snakiest people I have ever had the displeasure to meet where ghetto poor. Money does not make the person, its man that makes the money.

There are two basic uses for money:

1) Money can provide a comfortable life which will allow us time to develop our creative thinking

2) To render a service to others that outstrips our physical presence. In other words you could be asleep whilst your business is performing a service.

None of us really own ANY money because when we depart not a penny of that money comes with us. So it's not how much money we have that counts. It's what we do with that money whilst we have it.

Successful people understand that it takes another level of thinking to connect to the success zone. To enter that zone it's not money but a way of thought. For us to enter that zone, we must be ready to be mocked, maligned and misunderstood by those around us. Do we appreciate that ninety-five percent of the wealth in this world is owned by just one percent of the population. That means ninety-nine percent is fighting over just five percent of the wealth.

If you are living amongst the ninety-nine percent then of course you will seem different if you are now changing the pattern of your thought.

The ninety-nine percent will be asking you questions like why are you reading those books, why do you go to those meetings and why are you listening to that? You will be seen to be different by your very nature of wanting to excel. This is called thinking outside of the box. Schools don't teach children this so many of us spend our whole lives NOT thinking out of the box, and even sadder, not even AWARE that there is a box!

Growing up I hated art classes in school because I didn't think I was particularly creative. I also remember a time when I was so financially poor that I couldn't afford to buy a computer. If I needed even the most basic help, I had to ask others. Sometimes those I asked would make it seem like a great deal of expertise and time was required and I would feel guilty for asking them. However Alex, a good friend of mine, offered me a free home computer, taught me some of the basics and advised me to attend a very basic computer skills class. I only attended two or three times but I learned a great deal.

As time went by I became more proficient spending countless hours alone teaching myself via trial and error.

Soon I was doing things on the computer that most did not even know existed. I began creating my own workshops that wowed people.

The more I practiced the more artistic I became. It was then that I realised how much I loved art and how creative I really was.

The point I am making is that we sometimes make the wrong evaluations of ourselves then live by those evaluations.

These inaccurate evaluations imprison our true potential.

Since then I have had countless individuals and organisations asking me to teach them how to create artistic, professional presentations.

I've had trained ITC technicians tell me they have never seen someone use a computer the way I have. It also showed me that the same tasks I was asking others to help me on; I could actually do myself and probably do even better.

Opportunities exist all around us every minute and every hour of every day to increase our own awareness.

Many people believe that in order to be financially successful, you have to be at the right place at the right time. Whilst this is correct, there is a small part missing. You also have to be AWARE that you are in the right place at the right time.

I have been at the right place many times and didn't even know it. We need to become more aware of our opportunities in life.

They say that life moves in cycles; if this is true, then studying history is the both valuable and rewarding of all researches.

History can prepare you for today and help you plan for tomorrow.

I have been seriously studying history for the last thirty years of my life and if there was one thing I learnt from history, is that man does not learn from it. I advise all young people to learn from the past of your elders. Don't make the same mistakes of those who went before you.

One hundred percent of all power and energy exists everywhere one hundred percent of the time. How does this statement apply to you and me? The mobile phone has always existed but it took someone to discover the awareness of how to bring it out.

The Internet has always existed but it took someone to find the awareness of how to manifest it. Likewise your GREATNESS exists right now but it's whether you will find the time, will, technique and awareness to discover it.

No scientist can accurately say what you're capable of. That's down to you; you can create anything you want.

Now I can hear some of you saying Brother Andrew that's easy for you to say, but you don't know my circumstances! I come from a one-parent family ... I'm too dark, too short, too tall, I'm too poor or I was born under the wrong star. My reply would be to **SHUT UP**!!!! I'm not interested in your circumstances. Weak people blame circumstances for their failures.

Yet successful people do not live bound by circumstances. They create or change their circumstances to fit what they want in their lives. I'm sorry if this hurts but life can be brutally straightforward at times.

Life does not care about your personal circumstances – its totally neutral. You and I have the ability because we were created as supreme beings in this wonderful universe. Some of us are addicted to bad results because we have attached ourselves to bad circumstances.

We end up in jobs, organisations and relationships that we dislike yet we tolerate them, because we lack the awareness of how to transform ourselves. My advice is to surround yourself with what you want to become. If you associate with greatness it will affect you. You are worthy of true happiness and peace in your life, that is why you're here.

I really don't care about what mistakes you have made in life. The Creator forgives you. How do I know that you are forgiven? If you were not forgiven you would not be reading these words. You and I have the opportunity to set things right.

Let's take this opportunity with both hands. You are such a unique individual. Just be yourself. That is something that you can be better than anyone else.

Be yourself! Listen to that small inner voice that speaks to you from within and follow its guidance. In dark times that's your best friend and internal messenger.

NO ENEMY WITHIN

Try to obey it because it will warn and protect you from negative forces. I end by how I started with the ten magical, two letter words…

IF **IT** IS **TO** BE **IT** IS **UP** TO **ME**!

DAY 2 CHALLENGE

As Soon As You Wake Up	As soon as you wake up focus on what you would like to achieve for the day. Focus on the DETAIL, the colours, the feelings etc. then stand in front of a mirror and declare: "Today is going to be great, I Am phenomenal and today is going to be amazing" **Mini-Task:** Write a long list of your biggest failures. Remember what DID not work, this list will help you avoid past mistakes
Today's Mind-set Challenge	**Task Two – Let it go, Let it Go"** You have been this way for all your life and this is how far it has gotten you. For you to get to the next level of this game (called life) you need to give something up. For you to become the GIANT you were born to be, what baggage, what attitude and/or what habits are you going to let go of? There is something about **you** that is holding **you** back. **Today's** task involves you letting go and really focusing on what has been holding you back. If you know then write a short blurb about the impact cause, if you don't know, explore and look deep within. ***ALSO READ MINDSET CHALLENGE NUMBER 13 and put things in place so on this day you are ready*.**
Before You Go Sleep	Sit in silence for 10 minutes and **MEDITATE on the things you want – DO NOT LAY DOWN!** Input entry into diary or create voice note, Write - down any ideas **Prepare for tomorrow** SET YOUR ALARM CLOCK AND WAKE UP EARLIER THAN YOU PLANNED, at least 45 minutes earlier.

JOURNAL ENTRY

HOW WAS DAY 2?

Remember to challenge all negative forces

Describe your day. What went well? What do you need to improve on? What did you learn? Write as much as possible!

WELCOME TO **DAY THREE**

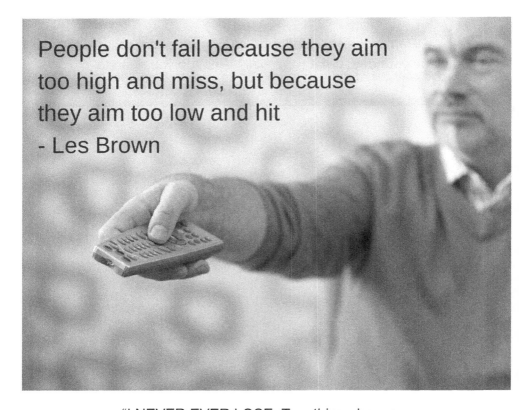

People don't fail because they aim too high and miss, but because they aim too low and hit
- Les Brown

"I NEVER EVER LOSE. Two things happen,
I either win or I learn, I never lose" Davis J Williams

It's time to UNLIMIT your POTENTIAL
By Julian Hall

Most people reading this are 'up', but not in a good way. They're fed 'up', putting 'up', fu%*ing 'up', some are locked 'up' physically or emotionally and some have lost their voice and shut 'up'.

Let me ask you – ARE YOU GOING TO GO OUT LIKE THAT?

Now anyone with an ounce of fight in them is going to say HELL NO…I'M NOT GOING OUT LIKE THAT…

BUT…

The question, is WHAT ARE YOU GONNA DO ABOUT IT?

Are you gonna get motivated by a few memes on your timeline and then go back to the same old BS that's been holding you back or are you going to take ACTION?

And this is the QUESTION that you need to ask yourself. What stops you from taking ACTION? It's not just about knowledge. I mean if it was we'd all be doing great.

There's an overload of information today.

If you're honest with yourself, you know what it is you need to do in order to take yourself to the next level. You DO but you just don't believe in yourself enough to take ACTION!

If I told you that I could help you to unlock your potential what would you say? You'd tell me where to sign up! You'd tell me that you're up to doing whatever it takes. But the truth is you're not. Not really. I could write down a list of exactly what you'd need to do in order to 'make it' but something, either in your past or present would stop you from doing it. You've gotten comfortable with being ordinary without even realising it,

Let's start right there. Did you know that when you were born that you had it all? You had everything you needed to DO IT BIG! You had LIFE!

As you grew up you were AMAZED by LIFE and ALL it had to offer. You were amazed by food, sights, sounds, learning, people and the air you breathed. You ran around experiencing as much LIFE as you could. And if you fell down, you may have cried for 5 minutes but you got up and started running around again without a care in the world.

When someone asked you what you wanted to be when you were a grown up, you said the first thing that came to your mind.

You said what you felt, not what you thought. What you said wasn't limited by who you were, where you grew up, who your parents were or what school you went to.

As far as you were concerned YOU COULD DO ANYTHING!

So what changed?

NOTHING! That's what! In fact, you're now in the position to do ANYTHING you want to. Because as a child you wanted to but couldn't. As an adult, nothing is stopping you.

Did you know that we're no longer six degrees separated from anyone? It's more like two or three. So whoever it is you want to meet, whoever it is you think can help you 'make it', anywhere in the world. You're probably only 2 or 3 degrees away from them!

Did you know that some of the most successful people started the fast track to their careers after the age of 40?

Did you know that there are more entrepreneurs under 21 than ever?

Did you know that we have access to more information than EVER in the history of man?

Did you know that all of this means that you have a greater chance of 'making it' than EVER before in the history of man?
Ok so the doom and gloomers are going to say different but fuck 'em…that's their reality, make yours different. You create your own reality, you ARE that powerful. If you want to believe that there are no opportunities then guess what? That's exactly what will happen. If you think that you're surrounded by opportunities then guess what, that's what's going to happen.

This isn't some spooky magic trick…nah. It's quite simple. If you focus on an idea then you'll see it more. Have you ever thought about buying a particular car or another thing you desire and all of a sudden you start noticing more of them? They didn't appear out of thin air. It wasn't magic. You just opened your mind to that 'thing' and now it's within your observational sphere of reference.

It's now a part of your reality!

Everyone has a secret to disclose about success. And the secret is that there's no secret. You've heard it all before. But it's going to take action not simply just listening.
It's going to take you bringing into your observational sphere of reference that which you want to attain.

If you bitch and complain or hang out with people who bitch and complain then all you're doing is reinforcing whatever it is you're bitching and complaining about. You're giving it energy.

Look, if what you've been doing so far has worked — keep doing it by all means.

BUT…

If what you've been doing hasn't worked then listen up! You become what you think about, it's that simple. If you think about becoming a billionaire day in, day out then at some point that's what will happen. If you constantly think about how tough things are then 'how tough things are' is what will remain. Remember, you have LIFE and that means you have all you need to make it happen. It all starts with thinking it, wanting it, feeling it and taking the appropriate action.

I'll see you at the top and we can enjoy the view together!

DAY 3 CHALLENGE

As soon as you wake up	Today's theme is forgiving and forgetting. **Forgiveness** IS NOT something you do for other people, **FORGIVNESS** is something you do for yourself so we can move on and grow. This morning, READ your promise letter with this in mind! Also focus on what you want to achieve today!!!
Todays Mind-set Challenge NOTE* You might have conflict with your family member; Now Enemy Within recognizes that this can be difficult. Live in the possibility of something better happening between you and that person instead of living in the negative past. Speak to your buddy about this***	**Task Three – "Bleach"** Go through your phone book and delete all the toxic people who are just not good for you. Search your environment and eliminate any toxic and negative influences, including pictures, old offensive emails anything, text messages etc. If you have OFFENDED anyone, or if there is tension between you and another EXTEND your arm so you can move in the right direction. Ask yourself, what would you like to be POSSIBLE?
Before You Go Sleep	**TONIGHT** you will dedicate to Les Brown, Eric Thomas or Rich Dad Poor Dad. Choose **One** on **YouTube**, Write a blurb on the following....**1)** What drives them? **2)** What are they about?

JOURNAL ENTRY

HOW WAS DAY 3?

Describe your day. What do you need to improve on? What went well? What did you learn? Write as much as possible!

WELCOME TO **DAY FOUR**

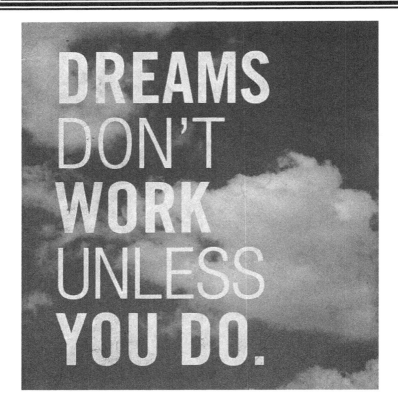

"This is your last chance. After this, there is no turning back. You take the blue pill — the story ends, you wake up in your bed and believe whatever you want to believe. You take the red pill — you stay in Wonderland and I show you how deep the rabbit-hole goes" ~ **Morpheus, 'The Matrix'**

"Are you a gazelle, or a lion - Part One?"
By Davis J. Williams

Once upon a time in the beautiful country of South Africa, a gazelle wakes up.

Sunrise ..."YAWNNNNNNNNN"

The lion wakes up and it understands that for it to survive it must outrun the animals that it hunts for food.

"YAWWWNNNNN"

A few hundred meters away a gazelle wakes up and it understands that for it to survive it must outrun the animals that hunts for food.

The main predator the gazelle must watch out for is the lion, the undisputed king of the savannahs. The gazelle's instinct and main focus is all about survival and he is committed to just that - surviving the day without being eaten. The gazelle knows the lion all too well; he knows that as soon as the sunrises, he better start running because as soon as the lion wakes up, he will be on the hunt.

NO ENEMY WITHIN

The lion's belly is now rumbling but it is all good because he sees a gazelle in the distance, it is at that moment that he is committed to getting his lunch, and lunch for his family who are still sleeping.

Here is the dilemma. For the gazelle to survive he must outrun the lion at all costs for if he gets caught, his life is over. The lion understands that if he is to feed himself and his family he must outrun the gazelle.

When the sun comes up, the gazelle starts running...and so does the lion!
Regardless of who you are in life, you have to run. You can either be the gazelle, running away from something or you can be the lion, running towards it. Regardless of your circumstance, you better start running.

What is the difference between the lion and the gazelle? Which animal would you rather be? Are you the animal running away from something or the animal that is running towards it?

Why is this even significant? Because when you're the gazelle and the lion isn't chasing, **you're not running**. But when you're the lion, you never stop running! you are always running to achieve your goal, always fired up, focused and patiently waiting for your reward. The lion is ultimately motivated by the WHY...which is greater than him and his personal wants.

The lion's reasons are powerful; nothing will make him oversleep or forget about feeding his family.

Regardless of the weather, circumstance or the day of the week the lion is driven by its desire to succeed in his quest. He is motivated is his family.

When the lion feeds, he does not eat the gazelle himself; he drags the dead corpse back to his family to feed on first. The lion is the bread-winner that is why he is the king of the animal kingdom.

The gazelle on the other hand has a totally different mindset to the lion. The gazelle doesn't run unless he has to. The gazelle is a loner who thinks only about himself. The gazelle, when he wakes up, does not run unless he is forced to run. The gazelle has no real motivation, drive or urgency.

In this world there are two types of people, the lion and the gazelle, those who are successful and those who are not successful, those who are driven by the goals and those who are not.

Understand this, everyone is successful. The person who works 9am till 5pm working in a dead end job grafting in an occupation that is hated with a passion IS SUCCESSFUL at just that...working in a dead end job. That is a success, not the success that was intended, but a success all the same. Johnny keeps getting in trouble at school. He keeps getting into arguments and fights and is constantly being sent home to an angry mother. Johnny is constantly told that he will not be successful. That is incorrect, little Johnny is already successful - at getting in trouble.

WELL DONE JOHNNY. What he doesn't know is that it does not have to be that way.

Johnny can create his own idea of what success is; all he has to do is create it through hard work and commitment.

In closing, if you want to be like the lion make sure you're prepared to run towards that which will feed you and your family and brings them joy. Lions love eating gazelles so the hunt must be an amazing experience for him. Make sure that whatever you are chasing is something that you are passionate about, something that brings you joy, happiness and satisfaction. Having this in place will ensure that your desire to succeed will override any urges to do nothing.

Now get up and run, run, run, run and catch that gazelle!

(Davis J Williams is a vegan and does not promote the hunting of any animal)

DAY 4 CHALLENGE

As Soon As You Wake Up	Mini Task - Commitment looks like WHAT? What is commitment? Before you get out of bed, take your phone and write a **list** of WHAT **things can one expect to see what someone is** COMMITED? Describe it in detail! Remember TO be **AWESOME** in everything that you DO….Don't settle for less
Today's Mind-set Challenge	**Task Four – APPEAR** Today you will create A VISION BOARD. Focus on the things you want and search for images that reflect that. Make it as amazing and creative as you want — Then attract it into your world! **Google** 'vision Board' for ideas and take a picture of the final design.
Before you go to sleep	Complete your journal and get ready to dominate tomorrow. Do 40 press ups or squats Create a voice note or video message of your experience so far. **Mini-task** Research 20 ways of making legit money, Google it, then present it to someone you know in need

JOURNAL ENTRY

HOW WAS DAY 4?

Describe your day. What do you need to improve on? What went well? What did you learn? Write as much as possible!

WELCOME TO **DAY FIVE**

"What you think, you become.

What you feel, you attract.

What you imagine, you create"

-Buddha

"If you're not able to take risks, you will never ever truly live. In order to take chances and prevail your fear, you must have **courage**, without it, you will never acquire the required confidence to grow out of your comfort zone"
~ **Muhammad Ali**

The Train
By Davis J. Williams

Picture this…

It was a Thursday night, 23.55 to be exact. The train was crowded as passengers made their way home from their late night adventures.

Those who had a seat sat quietly — some reading newspapers, some in thought, and others just resting with their eyes semi closed. I was one of the seat holders. The train was really calm and serene with nothing much going on. My eyes were closed, as I sat in deep thought miming my favourite song in my head.

> *"Get up, stand up! Stand up for your rights!"*
> *(Bob Marley, I just love that song)*

All of a sudden, a man and his children entered the train. There was one seat next to me that he occupied. His children stood by the doors. They were so expressive and boisterous that they transformed the whole environment of the train.

The man sat down next to me and closed his eyes, oblivious to the children's behaviour as they yelled and screamed, back and forth, bouncing into people and throwing items. It was chaos. Well it seemed like chaos to us. What a cheek I thought to myself! The man just sat there and did nothing.

I am not sure how he managed to do this because everyone else on the train was extremely irritated and frustrated by his noisy children.

I was getting to that point myself, as I could no longer concentrate on the lyrics of my favourite Bob Marley track. People around me were irritated and frustrated as they tried unsuccessfully to indirectly capture his attention. The person opposite me released the biggest cough ever to capture the dudes attention, but to no avail.

I was in no way threatened by this puny dude, so I had no doubts that I could get him to focus on his children, and create peace. Let me just wait for a few seconds to see if any of the other passengers gets his attention.

Being a 5 ft. 5" black male with an athletic build, gold teeth and wearing a hoodie can often be seen as intimidating to many especially those who are prejudice and media influenced.

I hoped someone else would step up and say something because I knew that if I asked politely, and he gave me any attitude, I would have knocked him out! A little extreme I know, but I was starving and needed some food and my ego was dying to get involved.

Three minutes went by and my patience and resolved impressed me, but enough was enough so I turned to him and said in my calmest voice ever (I did not want to insight any conflict)

"Excuse me … your children are disturbing a lot of people.
I beg you deal with them, take some responsibility" (followed by me kissing my teeth)

The man lifted his gaze as if becoming aware of the situation for the first time and said softly,

"Oh you're right. I guess I should do something about it.
We've just came from the hospital. We have been there all day, the boys just found out that their mother died. He looked at me and continued, "I don't know what to think, I feel totally numb and I guess they don't know how to handle it either, I am so sorry"

OMG (Oh My Gosh) I nearly crumbled…You can't imagine how I felt. As soon as he explained the situation my whole being changed; my whole energy towards them changed, I instantly transformed, even my hunger disappeared. Initially I couldn't stand them and to be honest I was ready to punch him up, but my point of view shifted and suddenly I saw things very differently.

I saw things differently because I looked at the situation differently. As the saying goes **WE DO NOT SEE THINGS, AS THEY ARE WE SEE THINGS AS WE ARE.**

Not only did I see things differently, I started to breathe differently, I thought differently, felt differently and therefore behaved differently.

My earlier complaint about the family vanished. I was no longer concerned about controlling his behaviour; my heart was consumed with the man's pain. Feelings of empathy and compassion flowed freely.

"I am so sorry about your loss. Please forgive me!"

We spoke for an hour on the train and then continued on the platform; and I ended up offering to help him by signposting him to various services that I was aware of that could help his children cope with their loss

I also shared my own experiences with him which then led to giving him my number to continue the conversation.

Some people waste days, weeks, months and even years falling out with people just because they think they know the full story. Their opinion is based on the limited information they have available to them and they make crucial life-changing decisions based on this. The worse thing is that we try and change people based on our limited knowledge. We can only transform our lives and our views of people when we quit focusing on the outer layers of attitude and unwanted behaviour and get to work on the root cause — the source from which all our attitudes and behaviours flow.

No enemy within — get to know yourself.

Last week someone asked me where do I get all my energy,

drive and positive motivation from…I thought for a moment

and said this -

"Every morning I wake up and remind myself that I have 24

hours left to live"

What would you do if you found out that you had 24 hours to live? Would you give everything 500%? Would you meet up with loved ones? Would you climb a mountain? Would you fulfill your dreams or pass them onto someone else? Would you instantly leave your stamp on the world? Would you shout out your passions for the world to hear? Would you be bulletproof? Unbeatable? Would your plans and actions be strong and unstoppable like titanium?

Live your next 24 hours like its your last….

#ihave24hourstolive

DAY 5 CHALLENGE

As Soon As You Wake Up	Wake up & declare today's goals in front of a mirror. Remind yourself of what you are committed to. **SPEAK IT LOUD & send it to your two SOLDIERS! Send to more if you want!! Remember the 2 SOLDIERS YOU recruited?** They are in your corner! Use them to stay strong! Make sure your goals are achievable and rewarding.
Todays Mind-set Challenge	**Task Five –** **In the Beginning was the word.** Today you will only speak positive words. This means not using limiting, disempowering words like **"It is impossible"** **"I can't"** **"That's long"** **"I'm tried"** **"I'll do it tomorrow"** **"I'm not good enough"** NO BUTS and NO EXCUSES! Instead, us words like **I can, I will** are advised. **This is not a priority** can replace I can't!
Before you go to sleep	Complete your journal and get ready to dominate tomorrow Do 40 Press Ups or Squats Create a voice note or video message describing your experience so far.

JOURNAL ENTRY

HOW WAS DAY 5?

Describe your day. What do you need to improve on? What went well? What did you learn? Write as much as possible!

WELCOME TO **DAY SIX**

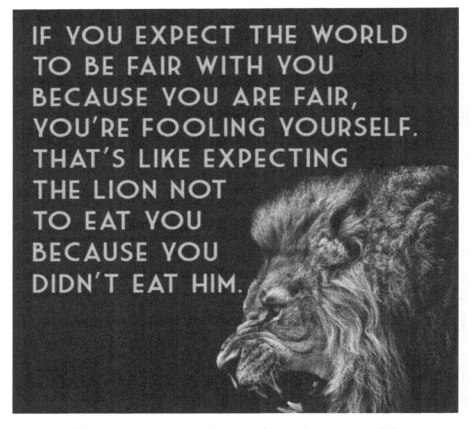

IF YOU EXPECT THE WORLD TO BE FAIR WITH YOU BECAUSE YOU ARE FAIR, YOU'RE FOOLING YOURSELF. THAT'S LIKE EXPECTING THE LION NOT TO EAT YOU BECAUSE YOU DIDN'T EAT HIM.

"The best way to predict your future is to create it."
Davis J Williams

DAVIS J. WILLIAMS

"If only you knew how important you are to me and I don't even know you."
By Leah Salmon, the *Naturally You* coach

Leah had an appointment with a client called P. One Tuesday evening, she called him ...

Leah: Hey P, how you doing?

P: I'm good, thanks for calling. What are we talking about this session?

Leah: Well, I have something really important to tell you today.

P: Sounds good, what is it?

Leah: P, do you want to know the most powerful thing you can EVER do?

P: Pass all my GCSEs?

Leah: No

P: Eat my greens and the crust of my toast?

Leah: No

P: Get a good job and make loads of money?

Leah: No

P: Become vegan and stop eating MSG and aspartame?

Leah: I like the way you're thinking, but no

P: Win a Mr. Strong Man competition?

Leah: Erm....NO!!!

P: Okay enough of the guesses, what is it?

Leah: P *(***dramatic pause and deep breath***)* The most powerful you can do in your WHOLE LIFE, is to acknowledge just how important you are to this world.

P: Okay Leah, what are you talking about?

Leah: A great man by the name of Paa Nabab Yaanun once said in his book *Your Potential*, that everyone may only have a certain amount of power, but everyone has unlimited POTENTIAL – which is your capacity to develop into something in the future, do you understand?

P: I'm with you so far, keep going.

Leah: So you can decide to become the best at anything you do and if you decide to be the best at anything, you instantly become very important; when you accept your importance you'll treat yourself very differently than you currently do.

P: Hold on, why does being the best at something make you important?

Leah: What do you want to become in the future, what's your life goal?

P: I've told you, I want to become an ultrapreneur, which is like a super entrepreneur in the clothing industry and a good parent, if I can find someone lucky enough to have my children.

Leah: *(chuckles)* ok so when you are the best fashion ultrapreneur around, who are you super important to?

P: Ummm I'm not sure, me I guess, I hadn't really thought about it

Leah: If you're the best fashion utrapreneur, you'll be important to your staff so they can earn a living. You'll be important to your clients so they get the best products or services from you, you'll be super important to your suppliers as your orders with them keep their business going, anyone else?

P: Yeah, I'll be important to my bank manager who'll get to hold all my money, I'll be important to my lucky partner and children to make sure they are well looked after, I'll be important to my designers as I'll help them get exposure for their design (pauses and thinks…) oh so if I'm the best fashion ultrapreneur, it makes me an important part of all of their lives, ahhh…okaaay …

Leah: Exactly and it doesn't stop there, your staff gets to work with the best; your trainees get to train with the best and you benefit from knowing you're doing the best.

P: Ok but what if I wanted to be a bus driver or a singer how is being the best at those important?

Leah: Anything you do to the best of your ability, will have the same impact on those around you as being a fashion ultrapreneur, being the best inspires motivates and energies everyone around you and you energise yourself by being the best you can be also.

P: Ok, I hear that but whether I think I'm important or not, I still treat myself pretty well

Leah: Ok, what did you eat today?

P: Cornflakes for breakfast and chicken and chips with a soft drink for dinner.

Leah: Junk food = junk thoughts and junk actions. Is this the way a top class VIP should feed their body? Is this the kind fof meal you'd serve to a VIP?

P: No probably not, I'd give them something good to eat

Leah: But you're a VIP too, so why don't you feed yourself like one, P? How much sleep did you get the last couple nights?

P: I was up on Facebook and Instagram till 3:30am then slept till 11am, then the night before I got in at 3am then had to get up 6am to go to work.

Leah: What would you have done if you were a VIP?

P: Probably got proper sleep, not been on Facebook or Instagram so I could wake up earlier to get started on my busy day.

Leah: Right! If you acknowledge that you WILL be the best at anything you decide to do, with some help and encouragement you'll start treating yourself with that same level of importance, from the clothes you choose to wear to how much water you drink and how much exercise you get, KNOWING you have the POTENTIAL to be the best will change you.

P: Ok, I get it, I get it, I'm the BEST

I know you can achieve anything, you are SO important to me already and I can't wait to see what you look like when you realise it too, take care and stay healthy, Leah

DAVIS J. WILLIAMS

DAY 6 CHALLENGE

As soon as you wake up	As Soon As You Wake Up Focus on what you plan to achieve for the day. Then stand in front of a mirror and READ your PROMISE LETTER. You should have memorise it by now!
Today's Mind-set Challenge	**Task Six – Mark My Words** Just like yesterday, today you will only speak **positive & powerful words**. This means that you cannot use limiting words like 'It is impossible, I cannot, that's long or I tried, I will do it tomorrow, I am not good enough, NO BUTS, NO EXCUSES! **INTEGRITY: In addition though, today you will DO EVERYTHING YOU SAY YOU WILL DO. Today you will HONOUR your word. Today you will remain amazingly awesome!** Watch how much you get done!
Before You Go Sleep	Complete Your Journal & Get Ready To Dominate Tomorrow Do 40 Press Ups or Squats Create a Voice Note or Video Message Of Your Experience So Far MEDITATE on your dreams for 10 minutes! That's right, sit in silence and focus on the things you dream of. Visualise in your MINDS eye all the things – SIT UPRIGHT – NO SLEEPING

JOURNAL ENTRY

HOW WAS DAY 6?

Describe your day. What do you need to improve on? What went well? What did you learn? Write as much as possible!

WELCOME TO **DAY SEVEN**

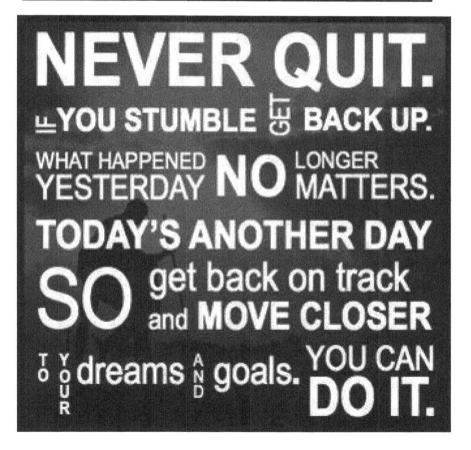

"FEAR is an acronym, F.E.A.R - False Evidence Appearing Real. The FEAR you have is not real; it just appears that way " **Michelle Thorney**

FREEZE! (Are you the Gazelle or the lion - Part 2)

By Davis J. Williams

There are some social constructs, Government agencies, organisations, and media campaigns whose sole purpose is to create wealth from your misfortunate. Trust me, they are passionate about preventing you from learning certain things about yourself and obsessed with making as much money as possible, regardless of how much blood shed and pain it causes.

TO THEM IT IS ONLY BUSINESS AND YOU ARE THE PRODUCT

It is *just* business, and in order for them to become a successful business they need you to be ignorant, obeying their regular commands and they need you to stay distracted and powerless.

For example, it costs on average £140,000 per year to lock up ONE young person in prison. Research shows that by locking someone up, the chances of them reoffending, being homeless and/or living in poverty are extremely high. So £140,000 is what it costs for one young person to go prison for a year.

Who pays?

The tax payers.

If £140,000 was invested in that young person's education, I am sure he/she would end up being a pilot, a doctor or even Prime Minister. In fact I am sure it would not even cost that much to support the young person, but that would be bad for business. If I owned a prison, behind closed doors, secretly, I would be happy to see my prison full.

It's called good business. If only young people knew the truth...hopefully they will know the truth now!

"Know the truth and that TRUTH shall UNFREEZE & MOTIVATE YOU"

You need to unfreeze yourself. Stop standing still.

Freeze, don't move, do nothing...freeze

Freeze!

Social Media says FREEZE! TV wants you to freeze, the music wants you to FREEZE

Social Media wants you to FREEZE!

Don't Move Buster!!!!!! Don't do anything unless we say so.

8am in the morning and already anti — social media bombards me with subliminal images and trivial gossip. It's only 8am!

Why am I being forced to watch Kim Kardashians fake booty, forced to watch adverts on TV of a dude wearing tight sexual shorts and heels selling car insurance, forced to buy tight jeans or the latest iPhone, which in my opinion is the most addictive phone on the planet.

The iPhone has the ability to render the most diligent student powerless to the constant tweets, updates and news feeds. I am looking at my iPhone now, look at it...it's so beautiful and gives me the ability to communicate with my friends, family or social networks in an instant. I am just connected to everything! What a buzz. I don't need to wait anymore, why wait? Why be patient?

'Go get it now' is the mantra that I see, hear and experience on a daily basis.

'Get rich or die trying' is a term used by many people as we strive to gain instant gratification, and damn the consequences.

The consequences are now getting out of hand. Look at the younger generation! I feel so sorry for them. When I was their age all I needed to focus on was playing conker fights, hide and seek, kiss chase, knock-down ginger, run outs and the other games that most young people today are totally unaware of.

These days' young people are under pressure to have the latest car, technical device, flashy jeans or latest handbag, believing these items somehow demonstrate that they have power and success.

With years of being told that they're not worth much and will never be worth much, I'm not surprised by their search for comfort in material things.

It seems as if we are living in a society that moves fast, one that is aggressive and competitive. It's dog eats dog out here!

Instant meals, catch up television, Sky Plus, microwaves, take away food, full time jobs, school, homework, parties, constant traffic, fights and arguments on social media, instant messages CONSTANT STIMULATION and 24-hour convenience stores all accelerate our lifestyles giving us little time stop, breathe and ask ourselves reflective questions like why am I doing this and why is it important?

We just don't have the time anymore; there's always something to do, especially when you got your trusted phone in your hands. The world is yours...or is it? WWW World Wide **WEB.**

There is that gazelle again. It escaped the lion's claws in part one (refer to day 4) because the lion caught another gazelle instead.

The brave gazelle decide to take a rest at a local water hole, quenching its thirst. The water hole was quiet so the thirsty gazelle decided to not only have a sip, but to also have a nice cool bath.

All of a sudden the gazelle looked up to see that massive, hungry, athletic lion was within striking range.

The gazelle was upset with himself, as he could not believe that the lion had gotten so close without him being aware of this. I guess he got caught 'slipping'.

Don't this lion don't ever rest? He is relentless, never phased by failure and this time he is looking even more confident than before, convinced that his family is sure to have a great meal.

The gazelle starts to panic, as he knows that this time he can't escape and that it's no use trying to run. The gazelle panics, desperately trying to find a solution to his potentially fatal situation. The gazelle calculates various escape routes, at lightning speed, and every bit of information that entered the gazelle's little brain screams danger, danger, danger, run, run, run, jump, escape, escape, help, help!

Regardless of all the stress the gazelle is going through there remains only 3 possible outcomes;

1) Shall I Fight

2) Shall I Run

3) Shall I Freeze

The gazelle, not being able to process all of that information goes into a state of hyper-arousal ... the over stimulation and influx of all that information forces the gazelle into a state of shock. **Hyper-arousal** is a state of increased psychological and physiological tension resulting in reduced pain tolerance.

Whilst the gazelle stands there thinking about what to do next the lion pounces and the gazelle is finally caught. It's really no match, so it doesn't even attempt to put up a fight. The gazelle's blood pressure drops. It gets colder and more rigid; it's ready to be eaten. At this point it freezes (hyper-arousal response), not moving a muscle; its heartbeat reduces, as does its temperature.

The lion, noticing these changes, thinks the gazelle is dead so decides to store it somewhere secure for future consumption.

The lion leaves the gazelle thinking it's dead, but of course it's not. Once the lion leaves the spot, the gazelle's heart rate increases and its body temperature rises and it escapes.

Humans have a similar response to the gazelle. We call it procrastination, or the freeze-response, where you have several things to do; yet you end up doing none. What was the main reason your laptop or mobile phone froze? It was over stimulated, too many applications opened at the same time.

I remember when I was at university studying for my degree, I was one of those students who would stay up late on a Sunday night working on a month-long assignment due the next day. I always have problems paying my bills on time NOT because I do not have the money BUT SIMPLY because I always get distracted or over stimulated by Snapchat, Instagram or Facebook.

Why do we willingly sabotage our success?

I am aware that I have been conditioned to be busy, always wasting my time building the dreams and legacy of someone else.

What makes it worse is that I always convince myself that everything is under control by saying that I work better under pressure simply to justify my substandard work by claiming if I had more time they could do better. Davis, FIX UP.

Are you like the gazelle? Just like the gazelles, human beings tend to **FREEZE** when they are terrified and feel like there is **no chance for our survival or no chance for escape** or if they think their future is doomed.

What are you afraid of? Why have you frozen?

"Do something today that your future self will say thank you for"

Can you relate to this story?

Are you constantly distracted and over stimulated with bad news (War, racism, blood shed etc.)

You may think you are, but maybe, just maybe you are doing what these corporations want you to do and being who they want you to be. Stop letting people control your emotions!

Who are you now and who are you going to be then?

Are you going to be the Lion or the Gazelle? Even though the gazelle escaped, will he escape the next time? He was lucky this time and he was lucky that the lion was not hungry himself.

Stop leaving your life in the hands of someone else, take control and know yourself, know who you are and create the change that you want to see.

Are you the **Lion** or the **Gazelle?**

'Who are you?' Is the most basic question one can ask but many of us struggle to give a good answer because what we end up doing is defining our status.

"Who am I?"

I am Davis J. Williams (I just told you my name. I am not my name. My name is the title that my parents gave me. I am not my name)

Some people define where they live (I live in Spain, London or Dominica), or what they have (I drive an Audi TT, I have a

BlackBerry or I own lots of properties), or they describe their character or profession (I am a doctor, I am down to earth, I am a lawyer, I am Peter the Plumber).

This is all well and good, but they do not define you; they simply describe what you do or what you have, not who you are 'being'. You are not even your name, when you were born you were nameless, but you existed. To successfully answer the question of who you are you must first strip yourself of all those labels and truly embrace who or what is left.

Imagine a graffiti artist who is about to spray paint onto a blank white wall. We are blank, until we create what we want to create for ourselves. Accepting this as a possible truth means that irrespective of what people think about us or what happens around us or to us, our core remains unchanged.

We remain focused and sure of ourselves; confident and untroubled. That is why it is your duty to ensure that there is NO ENEMY WITHIN. When your character is legendary and there is no enemy within, the enemies outside can never harm you. Through this journal I urge you to reconnect with your core, with who you really are and when you truly embrace that person you will notice that things around you will amazingly change, and remember, if you don't know where to start, create it yourself.. **TRY AND LIVE THE LIFE OF THE LION!**

WHAT HAVE YOU GOT TO LOSE?

On the 5th May 2005 I wrote a letter to success, this is what I had to say.

Success, how are you today? I just want to take a few moments to share how I feel about you.

I have been running away from you for many years, afraid of stepping up and claiming you but now I am ready. I want you so bad, I dream about you, I wake up in the middle of the night because of you, and I just can't stop thinking about you.

I don't want you because it will make me rich; I want you because it will make me a better person. I will hustle and grind for you. I know realise that it is only you that will make me happy.

I will make action a daily habit for you, I am willing to sacrifice for you! I might fear you but I wont quit until I get you. I don't want you for a minute, or an hour, I want you forever. I want to share you with my friends, my family, strangers everybody needs to embrace the fruits you have to offer. Success Success

You got me hypnotised, I know you will test me. I know you are fussy and that you have high standards and I am prepared to step up, I AM READY to man up and I AM going to prevail. I know that being good just wont cut it anymore; to get you I need to be GREAT, unforgettable and unbreakable. I now understand that you are not a car, a house, or thousands of followers on Twitter, you my precious success are a path, you are a journey, an attitude, a way of being and I promise to become one with you, I promise to think success, speak success, walk success, talk success and spread your theory to others. NO EXCUSES, NO DAYS OFF NO REGRETS.

DAY 7 CHALLENGE

As soon as you wake up	As Soon As You Wake Up Focus On What You Would Like To Achieve For The Day. Then Find A Mirror and READ your PROMISE LETTER. Memorise it
Today's Mind-set Challenge	**Task Seven – 3 for the price of 1** 1) Make a list of people who are most uplifting in your life and schedule time to spend with them each day (or as many as possible) 2) Face a fear head-on. Identify something you typically avoid doing and accomplish it in spite of the obstacles 3) Verbally acknowledge the strengths and virtues of those you love, really go out of your way and appreciate the people who have always been there for you.
Before you go to sleep	Complete your journal and get ready to dominate tomorrow Do 40 press ups or squats Create a voice note or video message of your experience so far **Mini-Task** Meditate on YOUR PURPOSE for 10 minutes (minimum) then **write** about what you **need** to do next.

JOURNAL ENTRY

HOW WAS DAY 7?

Describe your day. What do you need to improve on? What went well? What did you learn? Write as much as possible!

Congratulations!!!
You have completed 7 days of the detoxHD

WELL DONE!

You are now HALF WAY through. Keep on Grinding!
Look at how much you've achieved!

Imagine what another 7 days can do

WELCOME TO **DAY EIGHT**

"IF YOU ARE ALWAYS TRYING TO BE NORMAL YOU WILL NEVER KNOW HOW AMAZING YOU CAN BE."

Maya Angelou

"FEAR is an acronym:
F.E.A.R - False Evidence Appearing Real.
The FEAR you have is not real; it just appears that way"
Michelle Thorney

Never on schedule, ALWAYS on time

By Davis J. Williams

The year is 2014 and I am 38 years of age, soon to be 39 years old. That means that I have been on this planet earth for 38 years. 38 years, 456 months, 1982.74 weeks, 333101 hours, 1199163600 seconds, tick tock tick tock.

Regardless of what I have done in my 38 years, time has been tick tocking, tick tocking. It does not matter how powerful I am, how much money I accumulate, it doesn't matter how many followers I have on Twitter or Instagram, that clock will keep on tick tocking, as the saying goes

TIME WAITS FOR NO ONE

My life is my time, and my time is my life. You can lose money but make it back in the same instant by working hard, getting a new job or whatever, but once you lose time it is gone... forever.

People say that time is money...I disagree; TIME is LIFE, and what I do with my time will determine what my life will look like.

I was talking to a 15-year-old student in his final year of school, preparing for his exams. He had been in school since he was 5 years old, and the majority of his time/life has been spent in school, learning, adapting, remembering and growing.

He has spent more time with his teachers than with his own family and loved ones. He is now approaching his future-defining GCSE exams. Recently he disclosed to me that he has had enough of school and wanted to drop out. He said that he couldn't handle the stress anymore, couldn't tolerate the teacher's bulls**t, the early mornings or the huge expectation his family had of him. Within a space of four months his school attendance had dropped from an impressive 97% to a concerning 41%. His fall from grace had been so drastic that his school started having conversations about kicking him out of school permanently. This did not bother him because his actions demonstrated that he was prepared to QUIT, even though the finishing line was well within reach.

Imagine, quitting, surrendering, giving up...imagine going through pain, heartache, sacrifice after sacrifice only to receive no fruits from your labour. Normally people work hard and sacrifice to receive a reward at the end of their endeavours, but this lad had sacrificed ten years of his life and was prepared to receive NOTHING for it at the end.

This was something that I did not want to happen, so before I spoke to him about what had caused him to feel the way he did about school, I asked him one crucial question...

WHAT ARE YOU COMMITTED TO IN LIFE?

His response was predictable.

He thought for a moment before he replied

"I am committed to MONEY, success and my family"

So I then asked him

"What does commitment look like?"

The young man's left eye, swiftly followed by his right released a river of tears as he responded saying

"It looks like hard work, determination and...." He didn't manage to finish off his sentence.

If you feel like quitting, if you are not giving it 100% energy this short story is for you.

What are you committed to?

Are you committed to being ordinary or are you committed to being great? Commitment is the state of "being", who are you being?

Are you being a punk, a wimp, spoilt, a loser or are you being a winner, a champion, extraordinary and phenomenal. There are HUMANS and then you have the term 'HUMAN BEING'.

NO ENEMY WITHIN

Definition of ***human being*** in English: (**noun**)

A man, woman, or child of the species *Homo sapiens*, distinguished from other animals by superiormental development, power of articulate speech, and upright stance (Source: Oxford Dictionaries)

A Human BEING what???? Are you just a HUMAN or are you a Human being _____ ?(Fill in the gap)

Are you a human being lazy, are you a human being smart, are you a human being brave or are you a human being afraid?

You finish that sentence off for yourself!

Today I will be a HUMAN BEING...

What would your life look like if you fully embraced the possibility of being 100% committed to a cause?

No Enemy Within challenges you to embrace that commitment for 14 days.

Do you know how much your life would TRANSFORM if you did what you said you would do?

Commitment looks like action. Commitment is dressed up wearing workman boots with the laces tied up and a helmet, commitment looks like hard work, commitment looks like being busy working on your craft. Homer Simpson eating a jam donut is committed to being fat by way of his actions. .

If you want to make it in life, if you want a productive life you need to show commitment to that. Your life will be busy and active but the results will be mind-blowing.

Commitment is a massive word, commitment is a word that many use but don't embrace.
When it comes to commitment there are **NO** grey areas, there is no sitting on the fence. You are either committed or not.

So what are you committed to?

Are you committed to living a life that brings you nothing but bad news, stress and annoyance or are you committed to a life of happiness and wealth? The indication of your commitment is what you do with your **time**. What you do with your time directly reflects what you are truly committed to. There are people who say that they are committed to being the best footballer, or owning a business but they spend their time sitting on their laptop posting statuses of how great they are. If that is you, understand this, you are not being true to yourself, you are being fake, why be fake when **greatness** is within you? There you are, reading these words, I don't even know you, but I can guarantee this ONE thing, you HAVE

GREATNESS WITHIN YOU. *No Enemy Within* is about ADDRESSING that little voice in your head telling you to be ordinary, telling you to live a life that no one remembers. IT IS TIME TO COMMIT TO YOURSELF and what you really want. You are either committed to being successful or you are committed to pretending to be successful. As Nike says, **JUST DO IT**.

OOOiii!!!! Did you just say that you would TRY your best? Don't try!
You cannot TRY and be committed. The word **TRY** is a CON, a TRICK, and using that word means nothing. TRYING TO DO SOMETHING MEANS NOTHING. You are either committed or not.

If you are trying to be committed that means you are not! Being committed means that you are not going to make any excuses whatsoever, regardless of how hard it is. Last week I wanted to go jogging, I looked out of the window; I saw snow and went back to bed. Being committed means going jogging regardless of the weather. Being committed means that your character, your focus and your intentions cannot be compromised. Being committed means that you DO WHAT YOU HAVE TO DO UNTIL IT IS DONE.

Being committed to using the time you have to serve you, instead of you serving time. Time is your most precious asset, name one thing that is more valuable than time.

You cannot stop time, you cannot replace time, the only thing you can do is use time effectively. All work requires time and the better you are at using your time the more rewards you will get from your labour.

We all have the same 24 hours to use to the best of our ability. When you compare the world's wealthiest person and yourself one of the main differences is how you use the time you are given. You have ten fingers, so do they. You both have the same potential but the only difference is that they have self-belief and they INVEST their time in the right area whilst others waste their time. Imagine having the world's most precious asset and giving it to people you don't like. That is madness, but that is what many people do. They give their valuable time to people they hate, dislike or don't really want to be around. STOP IT. IT DOESN'T MAKE SENSE.

To ensure that you use your time as effectively as possible it is always best to:

1) **Plan your day**. Have a guide and ensure that this plan is in line with whatever you are committed to.

2) **Learn to say no**. Many times we find ourselves doing tasks for people that we didn't plan to do, we just somehow get tricked into pleasing other people and never putting ourselves first.

3) **Spend your time, don't waste it.** Start using the world's most valuable asset, TIME. Some people waste time like it's nothing. How do you spend your time?

Finally:

STOP SAYING THAT YOU'RE TOO BUSY. By claiming to be always busy means that you can't possibly do anything else. Instead of declaring you're too busy or don't have enough time, try declaring it's not a priority for you right now and see how that feels. Changing the relationship we have with time reminds us that anything is possible.

Time is a choice. If we don't like how we're spending our day, we have the power to change it. Saying the 'I'm so busy' becomes a mantra and that mantra becomes a self-fulfilling prophecy. If you're constantly telling yourself and others that you don't have the time or that you're up to your eyes with work, you will create that possibility in your future. If a judge in court can make time, you too can. Learn how to make time, just like a judge

Yesterday's the past, tomorrow's the future, but NOW is a gift. That's why it's called the present.

How to MAKE your OWN Day / Design a day

When I was young I was always taught that we had 7 days in a week, Monday to Friday and every day consisted of 23 hours, 6 minutes and 6 seconds, rounded up to 24 hours. This is common sense to many, but what I did not realise is that we have the ability to create another day.

We are now living in a society that has been sped up, FAST FOOD, INSTANT MESSAGES (emails, Whats App, text etc), Catch Up Television on Demand…everyone is racing around, busy busy, busy busy (read the essay FREEZE by Davis J Williams)

I was listening to the album 'How to pimp a butterfly' by Kendrick Lamar and there was a section where Kendrick was explaining that a **judge makes time**. That is right, judges make time when they sentence someone to a period behind bars. This made me think. Not only was I told that there was only 7 days a week, but I always hear my friends and family wish for more time.

"I didn't have time to focus on my dreams, I was too busy"

"I wish there were more days in the week so I could do the things I want to do"

We really have to start claiming our time back, creating time, like judges so we don't have to make such statements like "there is not enough time"
To create time, to design a day, all you need to do is follow these 3 easy steps.

Step 1)

Wake up early. We tend to wake up at a time our masters dictate. We allow just enough time to wake up, get ready and do whatever it is we need to do like work, school etc. Explore the possibility of waking up early. 1 or 2 hours early every day, and use those hours to do the things you HAVE TO DO. FOCUS on yourself. No chores, no contracts, no DIY, FOCUS on you, your dreams and your desires.

Step 2)

Ease off social media as we **spend** way too much **time** on there.

Step 3)

Go bed later, 1 to 2 hours later and follow step 1. If you need a nap, take a nap during someone else's time, but whatever you do, stop sleeping on your dreams.

Without realizing it, you have just made time. All you did was wake up earlier and went bed later. These changes might seem small at first, but over time WILL HAVE an enormous change in your life. Seeds start off small, but with the right nurturing and attention has the potential to become an OAK tree, or an amazing human being. So there you have it, you have made an hour here, two hours there, 30 minutes etc, when you calculate all the time that you have accumulated over the days, it will soon add up to 24 hours, your designer day, your very own day that you made! Forget 7 days in one week, you can have 8 or 9 days in your week and never again will you run out of TIME. Some people waste money. Some people waste time. Some people spend money, some people spend time, and some people make money, now you can start making time. Stop letting other people TELL you what you must do with your time. I know its hard, especially if you are attached to society, with its rules and structures, the 9am to 5pm cycle, all work and no play, its time to turn the tables. You are the master of your destiny; you control your time and what you do with it.

DAY 8 CHALLENGE

THIS IS DAY 8, ITS TIME TO UP THE LEVELS!

As soon as you wake up	As soon as you wake up focus on what you would like to achieve For the day. Then find a mirror and READ the PROMISE LETTER that you have Memorised.
Today's Mind-set Challenge	Today you will prepare for **DAY 9.** On **DAY 9** you will survive with no money or cash cards in your pocket. Leave it at home. Prepare for a packed lunch, drink and snacks. Learn not to spend any money in any shop! **TODAY** HOWEVER you will create your personal S.W.O.T breakdown. **S** stands for Strengths, **W** are your weaknesses,, **O** stands for Opportunities and **T** stands for threats. Really focus on each area and write a few words. Once you have finished put a plan in place to transform things in your favour. Also SHARE YOUR PROMISE LETTER WITH **5** PEOPLE! Don't delay! Let's go, let's go, move fast before that ego has something to say.
Before you go to sleep	Complete your journal and get ready to dominate tomorrow. Do 40 Press ups or Squats Create voice note or video message of your experience so far Meditate for 10 minutes whilst sitting upright and focus on how you are going to improve tomorrow.

JOURNAL ENTRY

HOW WAS DAY 8?

Describe your day. What do you need to improve on? What went well? What did you learn? Write as much as possible!

DAVIS J. WILLIAMS

WELCOME TO **DAY NINE**

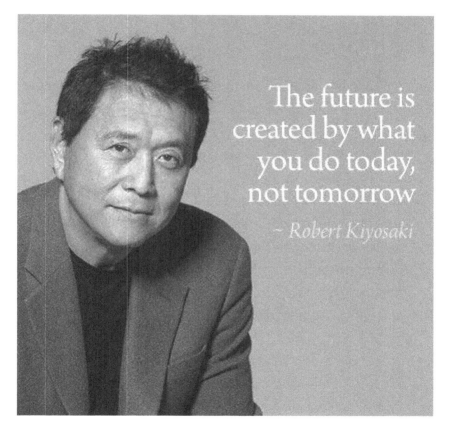

The future is created by what you do today, not tomorrow

~ *Robert Kiyosaki*

"The richest people in the world look for and build NETWORKS. Everyone else looks for work" **Robert Kyosaki**

Star Synergy
By Candice Bryan

Notice how each star holds its position on a clear dark night. But when looked at in relation to other stars surrounding it, that solo position becomes a collective picture reflecting symmetry, patterns and other creations, but only when looked at as a collective of stars…

"Discover who you want to be, before you discuss what you want to do."– Kubi Springer, 2015

We are often told we must study a particular subject, to master a trade or qualify in a specific discipline. Without exploration, wonder and research, how would we discover what our special "ism" might be? If you're still wondering and feeling uncomfortable about finding that one talent don't be fooled into accepting that you have only one thing that can make you shine brighter than you already do. You have a variety of skills and talents! At times we just don't realise!

"Out of many, we are one" – Bob Marley
"One hand can't clap" – Jamaican Proverb
It's a beautiful journey to be able to research and explore who you want to be, so long as you share your findings with others later.

Along the way it would be an equally great opportunity for you to identify which of your talents can also help you create a legacy of wealth. Exploring your talents and applying the natural skills you have with others can help you to grow and may even help you decide what it is you would like to do). Taking time to discover your talents could help you influence the use of your talents by others.

Information represents only the potential for power. Just like the power in a light bulb is realised only when it is connected to a circuit, information lacks power until it is connected into a network and used by its owner"
– Dr Claud Anderson (Powernomics, 2001)

Just think about the person who gave you this book or how [No Enemy Within] has come to be in your possession. That person or avenue is part of a rich network that can help you apply your talents. After all, shouldn't research resolve with some sound recommendations? That inner voice that may have had you doubting for some time, may just need to verse with wise counsel and positive vibrations. Who better than those other stars who are hidden in your immediate network of people?
We are constantly growing and changing, just like the seasons and learning from others.
So allow yourself to be open to the beautiful reflecting qualities of other stars around you!

People think that in order for something to work, it has to be complicated, but a lot of times the opposite is true. We usually attain success by putting the simple truths that we know into practice. "The basis of any struggle is people coming together" - Assata Shakur (Autobiography, 2014)

When you are ready to reach out to those in your network, or share and invest in your talent imagine your light will shine bright! Fill yourself like with enough fuel, positive vibrations and a mindset that will take you to the next level. When you work in synergy with others like stars do on a dark night, the pictures created can be truly magical. Through research, partnerships and mini personal projects you are sure to discover just which one of your many talents you will choose to begin creating your wealth!

To be **successful** you must be willing to, at any moment, **sacrifice** what you are, for what you will **become**.

As a child you stood out, it's time to relive that now and then for the rest of your life!

DAY 9 CHALLENGE

As soon as you wake up	As soon as you wake up ask yourself what your excuse is. Why haven't you been pushing yourself? Why are you settling for less? Today you are going to give it 200% effort
Today's Mind-set Challenge	**Task 8 – BRANDING-** We are all aware of Brands like Apple, Sony, Nike, Davis J Williams or Google and what these BRANDS stand for but have we ever looked at ourselves as a BRAND? **A PERSONAL Brand** is the name, term, design, symbol, or any other feature that MAKES YOU STAND OUT from everyone else. We all want to stand out, well, that was the deal when we was young and BRAVE ☺ Today's theme is personal branding. Your task is to create your very own Mission statement, a purpose, a vision, a slogan, a logo, a problem you are trying to solve. Many people use Instagram to BRAND THEMSELVES. Facebook and Twitter help people brand themselves to the world. But social media is not real. TODAY you will let your creative juices flow and turn yourself into a BRAND. Give as much detail as possible. Your BRAND should make you stand out from the crowd! Develop a slogan, a logo, do some research. Put pen to paper.
Before you go to sleep	Before you sleep close your eyes and picture yourself in the house of your dreams. What are you wearing? What country are you in? What can you smell? Who are you with? What music is playing in the background? How did you get there? Write 1 A4 PAGE explaining AND link it to your BRAND!

JOURNAL ENTRY

HOW WAS DAY 9?

Describe your day. What do you need to improve on? What went well? What did you learn? Write as much as possible!

DAVIS J. WILLIAMS

WELCOME TO **DAY TEN**

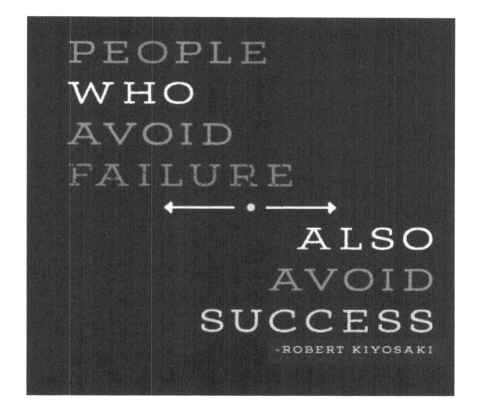

"Our deepest fear is not that we are inadequate. OUR DEEPEST
FEAR IS THAT WE ARE **POWERFUL** BEYOND MEASURE"
Coach Carter

Embrace F.E.A.R

By Michelle Thorney

Has anyone ever told you how fantastic you are? Have you ever looked in a mirror and reflected on the fact that there is only one you? There is nobody out there like you! Try it.

In life there are so many 'what ifs', there will always be a reason or excuse as to why we can't do something. In fact, the biggest reason that we don't do so many things is FEAR.

But what are we really afraid of?

1. Not being good enough

2. Being rejected

3. Failure

Ok, this is usual, but now ask yourself what's the worst thing that can happen in each of those situations? How are you going to know whether you're good enough if you don't try? When you feel rejected what do those people who make you feel like you are being rejected mean to you? If nothing why do you care? In life you are always going to make mistakes but true failure is when you fall down and refuse to get back up.

I want to let you know that you are amazing and I see the full potential in you and I hope you see it to. You can do anything you put your mind to and the only barrier is you.

All of the answers are within you, so don't be so hard on yourself. Stop focusing on all the negative things that are going on in your life because they don't define you as a person, they are just the things that have happened to you. You are so much more than that. Focus on the positive things in your life and know that you have the power to bring about the changes you want to see.

Keep on pushing and don't let FEAR - *False Evidence Appearing Real* - win.

The reason I am saying this is because I was once you. I was that person who put everything off until tomorrow or always had an excuse as to why I chose to stand still. I told myself stories that I had created about myself like "you can't apply for that job Michelle, you're not good enough" or "you won't get it because you're not good at public speaking and who is going to listen to you anyway?"

The older I got the worse it became because I was in my own little bubble/comfort zone and I thought I liked it there. The change came for me when a friend of mine pushed me to go for a job interview in housing.

I really didn't want to go because I had already told myself I wouldn't get it because I didn't have experience in that field and 'it's long'. I was stressing out and venting to my partner about why I shouldn't go for it and he said something that was like a light bulb moment to me. He said, "why you stressing out? What have you got to lose? And what is the worst that can happen?"

I couldn't answer him; he was right. What is the worst that can happen? It's either I get the job or I don't, simple. So I just told myself to fix up and went to that interview with confidence!

After I finished the interview the sense of achievement felt fantastic. I said to myself that even if I didn't get the job I wouldn't care. It just felt good pushing myself out of my comfort zone; it felt so refreshing and I felt in control, like I had regained my power. Crazy I know, but to cut a long story short I received a call at the end of the day telling me that I'd got the job. Since then I have tried to adopt that same 'what have I got to lose' attitude in everything I do and I have gone from strength to strength. Right now I have my own business called BeYoutiful Beginnings, a female empowerment program that delivers workshops to young females. Don't be afraid to step out of your comfort zone, because that is where your greatness lies. Good luck and remember F.E.A.R is simply

False **E**vidence **A**ppearing **R**eal

DAY 10 CHALLENGE

Today's Mind-set Challenge	ROLE PLAY: Today you will act like **YOUR BRAND** for the duration of the DetoxHD Challenge. You will act in accordance to your massive mission and will infect others also with your excitement brand. Talk about it, share it and live it.

Tonight ponder on this and really grasp the lesson:

"Understand: people judge you by appearances, the image you project through your actions, words, and style. If you do not take control of this process, then people will see and define you the way they want to, often to your detriment. You might think that being consistent with this image will make others respect and trust you, but in fact it is the opposite—over time you seem predictable and weak. Consistency is an illusion anyway—each passing day brings changes within you. You must not be afraid to express these evolutions. The powerful learn early in life that they have the freedom to mould their image, fitting the needs and moods of the moment. In this way, they keep others off balance and maintain an air of mystery. You must follow this path and find great pleasure in reinventing yourself, as if you were the author writing your own drama" **50 Cent,** *The 50th Law*

JOURNAL ENTRY

HOW WAS DAY 10?

Describe your day. What do you need to improve on? What went well? What did you learn? Write as much as possible!

WELCOME TO **DAY ELEVEN**

"Have you ever known anyone to write a plan on how to be lazy, overweight or poor?" **Davis J. Williams**

DAVIS J. WILLIAMS

Where you come from, doesn't have to be where you end up
By Warren Ryan

They say knowledge should acquired then passed on. So this is my gift to you. What I am about to tell you will change your entire life.

I was told from a very young age, that the only person who can save your life is you. If you are reading this right now, you are doing just that. It's 2015, and as I sit and write this, it is 972 days since I have found my purpose in life. During this time I have invested in myself every single day so that I can live life on my terms, regardless of the adversities I have faced throughout my life. It all starts with the mind. First I had to break it down so I could understand exactly how the mind works. You see, how you see the world right now, isn't how the world really is. My old beliefs devalued me as a person; I had to go from feeling like just a number, to feeling like one of a kind. I am 1 in 7 billion, just like every one of us. The masses are conditioned to feel like they are just a number in this world. I had to reprogram my mindset, just like a laptop with new software. That is when I started to live life on my terms. A life with no limitations.

I am 'The Mind Mechanic' of the UK. I run two businesses that I created, so I get paid for doing something that I love.

This is what wakes me up before my alarm clock. My passion is adding value to people's lives. I have attained a following of over 50 thousand strong followers through social media. I run self-development events across the UK. The goal is to create my first million followers before 2019 so I can touch millions of lives. I give people the tools to take control of their emotions, which determine their actions, through tailoring their thought process, because what you think determines how you feel. In a short space of 972 days, my words have reached out to thousands of people and literally changed their lives. From people suffering with deep depression, to professionals who need to step up to the next level. If you want to live the life you have always wanted, you must first fine-tune your map so that your vehicle gets you to your destination.

Your route will come up against roadblocks both physically and mentally, but you have the tools to overcome anything in life because it's not what happens to you, it's what you do about it. It depends how you look at the roadblocks of life; you can let them break you, or let them add value to the person you already are, because you will go straight through these road blocks to get to where you need to be.

Henry Ford said, "There are those that think they can and those who think they can't. The funny thing is they are both right." My life is living proof that where you once came from, doesn't have to be where you end up.

Let me take you back to the start. I was brought into this world by a 17-year-old single mother who was addicted to drugs. By aged 8, I was father to my three younger siblings, who were eventually separated and split up into different foster homes. I was constantly bullied for my disheveled appearance, my situation at home and not having a father. Going through all of this resulted in a lot of anger and pain that I kept bottled up inside of me. Yet, even by the age of 13, I knew I wanted to be someone important in this world and use this struggle to do something good, I just didn't know how. I thought that to be significant, I should put my talent in football to use and become a footballer. This came true at 16 when I had an opportunity to play for Bristol Rovers Academy. I had the ability to go far but it was the mental side that was letting me down.

At the age of 19, I was released from Bristol Rovers and I was devastated. I soon fell into a toxic relationship; this was the final piece of what was going to be my toughest challenge to overcome. Depression (the silent killer) consumed me and I hit rock bottom. All the trauma from my past that I had bottled up, came to the surface. This was the first time I had ever thought about taking my life.

DAVIS J. WILLIAMS

I couldn't see any way out. I had a decision to make; do I take anti-depressants, or do I find the root cause. It was at this time that I had been offered the opportunity to work in America.
This was perfect timing for me to find the root cause of the depression.

I knew I would have to dig deeper into my mind to unlock the answers that I was looking for and to overcome this demon that was taking over me. I became obsessed with how the mind works, understanding how emotions are created, how life experiences and surroundings have a profound effect on how you feel. Once I worked out that what you think determines how you feel, I changed my whole thought process to only look for the good in every situation. I realised that what you repeatedly do, you become.

There was once a time when you couldn't walk, but you practiced it repeatedly until you mastered it. This repetition created a programme, which allowed you to walk on autopilot. The same process applies to any task. I had to have laser focus. Once the root cause was found, I found the secret to success, it was like I found my true identity by getting to know the real me.

That is when I decided that I needed to pass this knowledge on by becoming a Motivational Speaker.

I flew back to the UK a year later with the drive to change the mentality of the masses.

The aim was to move from Bristol to London. Thing is, I only had £400 to my name. I knew that this was a sink or swim situation and sinking wasn't an option.

I found a cheap box room to rent, but I didn't mind as this chapter in my life was going to lead me to greater things. I went to schools, colleges and anywhere I could be of value to people. I worked for free believing that they would book me again and pay me once they knew the value I could bring.

I surrounded myself with leaders and wealthy people so that it came normal for me. Soon enough I was going on radio stations and TV shows sharing my story. I was starting to build a reputation in London and became known as 'The Mind Mechanic'.

I was mentoring people from all ages and walks of life. I decided to create an event called 'Prove You Exist' with the aim of bringing unity and knowledge to the people. I was being recognised for my work and the value I was adding to people's lives. I was then nominated for an inspirational award at the BAFTAs, which I won.

I have since started two companies; *Need 4 Success* business partner called and my own brand *Warren Ryan the Motivational Speaker.*

The formula for success comprises of six key principles, which form the foundation my company *Need 4 Success.*

These six principles are;
- Know Your Worth
- Know Your Why
- Give Back
- Your Goal
- Erasing Fear
- Gratitude

To programme these key principles, requires repetition of affirmations, visualisation, reading and listening to relevant educational content and most importantly, action. All of these must be applied with emotion to have the most significant effect on the mind. It takes 21 days to create a new habit; so practicing this repeatedly sets a new mindset so you can live life on your terms. All the great athletes, actors, inventors and entrepreneurs share these same principles.

The subconscious mind is what I like to call the mother mind. It controls your habits, your beliefs and actions.

When this mind is formed it is open, so the surroundings and the people that surround that child programme the subconscious mind to think and behave in a certain way.

From the age of four, your conscious mind is created. This is the intellectual mind. It has the ability to accept and reject. It will play in harmony with the subconscious mind.

So for example, if your parents were athletic, the likelihood of yourself having similar abilities is fairly probable. The same if applies if you're brought up around crime.

The subconscious mind is 30,000 times more powerful than the conscious mind. It determines how you see the world and your perception. Two people could be in the exact same situation, one could love life, and the other could hate it. All depending on how they view life.

If you don't control your mind, someone else will. That is why people fall into every day jobs. The very few that live life on their terms, are the ones that condition their own mind.

The secret to live a fulfilled life, is mastering the mind.

DAY 11 CHALLENGE

As soon as you wake up	Focus on what you would like to achieve for the day. Then find a Mirror And READ your PROMISE LETTER. Refer to your BRAND and remind yourself how you need to act
Today's Mind-set Challenge	**SELF TALK -** Muhammad Ali said that he was the greatest. That was his mantra; he said it so frequent that his opponent also believed that he was the greatest! Today you will create 5 mantras (i.e. 'I can do this' or 'I am awesome' and 'Unstoppable' etc.) these mantras you will write down and say as often as possible. EVERY POSSIBLE moment you have you will remind yourself that you are great, or whatever your affirmation said. Feeling in doubt? Physically reach for your affirmation and read it. Tired? Where's your affirmation? Got a deadline? Affirmation…
Before you go to sleep	Have a conversation with your mum, dad or loved one and share your day. Share the benefits of this DetoxHD. Complete your journal and get ready to dominate tomorrow. Do 40 press ups or squats Create a voice note or video message of your experience so far.

JOURNAL ENTRY

HOW WAS DAY 11?

Describe your day. What do you need to improve on? What went well? What did you learn? Write as much as possible!

WELCOME TO **DAY 12**

"Life is not about FINDING yourself it is about

CREATING yourself" -**Viv Ahmun**

DAVIS J. WILLIAMS   161

G Code
By Swiss (So Solid Crew)

I'm going to share with you three of many G codes that my friends and I learned over the years growing up in the hood. Being a G isn't about doing what's bad; it's about doing what's right. Real G's learn from other people's mistakes.

G CODE 1
REAL G'S KNOW THEY'RE MOST POWERFUL WHEN THEY USE THEIR MIND.
You can create anything with your thoughts. A thought created the book you're reading right now **My G**. Every great idea was once a thought, SO BELIEVE IN YOUR ABILITY TO THINK GREAT AND THINK BIG. I don't care what results you got in school, because those results don't mean you can't have a good, successful future.

You can be anything you think about being, but don't leave it too late, BE GREAT NOW! Always think before you act because when you don't think first, you suffer later. Be wise with your thoughts and when you want to get things done, always focus on what you want rather than what you don't.

G CODE 2

REAL G'S CONTROL THEIR EMOTIONS.

In life, but especially in the hood, it's important to control your feelings. If there's anything that gets us into negative situations most, it's our reaction to our feelings.

Just because you feel some type of way, it doesn't mean you have to react to it. **All My REAL G's** know every reaction has a consequence. So every feeling MUST be thought about, this is a very important **G CODE**. Feeling without thought means there's no direction, and no direction brings problems. Make sure you can see where your feelings are leading you **My G**. Be focused, stay focused!

G CODE 3

REAL G'S CONTROL THEIR TONGUE.

Lil Wayne said "**Real G's** move in silence like lasagne". Know when to be quiet **My G**. You don't have to say everything you're thinking; focus on what you need to do to become great and speak only about important things in life. Don't waste time talking about people and spreading rumours.

The more you talk the less you get done, the more you get done the less you talk, another important **G CODE**.
Real talk and real G's respect it!

Remember

- Your thoughts can create anything
- Every great idea started as a thought
- A bad past doesn't mean you can't have a good future
- You can be anything you think about being, if you work hard
- Think before you act
- When you don't think first, you suffer later
- Focus on what you want, not what you don't want
- Control your feelings and emotions
- Don't create problems unnecessarily
- Feelings without thought means there's no direction and no direction brings problems
- Know when to be quiet
- You don't have to say everything you're thinking
- Don't waste time speaking about people and gossiping. The more you talk the less you get done, the more you get done the less you talk.

DAY 12 CHALLENGE

As soon as you wake up	Focus on what you would like to achieve for the day. Then find a Mirror And READ your PROMISE LETTER. Refer to your BRAND and remind yourself how you need to act
Today's Mind-set Challenge	**Tie it up -** Today you will tie together all the loose ends that you have. The tasks that you have been running away from, the unsaid conversations with your friends or loved ones that you have been avoiding.. Today it ends and you complete everything! THEN…you will share your GOALS and PURPOSE with as many people as possible. INVITE PEOPLE INTO YOUR WORLD.
Before You Go Sleep	Complete your journal and get ready to dominate tomorrow. Do 40 press ups or squats Create a voice note or video message of your experience so far

JOURNAL ENTRY

HOW WAS DAY 12?

Describe your day. What do you need to improve on? What went well? What did you learn? Write as much as possible!

DAVIS J. WILLIAMS

WELCOME TO **DAY 13**

"DEATH IS NOT THE GREATEST LOSS IN LIFE. THE GREATEST LOSS IS WHAT DIES INSIDE WHILE STILL ALIVE. NEVER SURRENDER."

"The question is not CAN YOU…..the real question is WILL YOU? Is your WHY bigger than your WHY NOT?" –
Davis. J. Williams

DAVIS J. WILLIAMS   167

The Sentence
By Davis J. Williams

One of the challenges of DetoxHD is not using the words **can't**, or **impossible** and phrases like **I am tired, it's long, I will do it another day or it's too hard.** *No Enemy Within* understands the impact of these words and that is why we have dedicated this section to the power of words.

To many people, words are innocent, powerless and random. Many of us learned to speak by listening to our parents who learned from parents who learned from theirs. But rarely do people fully study words and their origins.

Words (language) are more than a tool for communication. We perceive our world through words. Those who read the Bible understand the power of words and how words create.
'In the beginning was the word'

JUICY PINEAPPLES

Before you saw the word *pineapples* you didn't think about it did you? Words create! (Did you taste a pineapple?)

In the 1990's Dr. Masaru Emoto performed a series of experiments observing the physical effect of words on water.

Dr. Emoto had photographers take pictures of water after being exposed to the different words then froze the water so it would form an ice/crystal like structure. The results were nothing short of remarkable. Every time Dr. Emoto exposed the water to positive words and then immediately froze the water the photograph taken of the structure of the ice would always be beautiful and symmetrical. However, when he exposed the water to negative words the water crystals would be disfigured and chaotic.

Considering we are made up of 70% water, you can see that sticks and stones may break your bones, but words can indeed harm you!

It is obvious how certain words can demotivate and disempower.

"I can't do this"

"This is long"

"I hate waking up in the morning"

"Why try when I will only fail?"

Saying these words not only demotivates you but it actually affects your body, especially when you say them with passion, conviction and emotion.

By changing the way you refer to yourself you start to change the way you see yourself and the world around you. You can start by rephrasing the way you say things – for example:

"I can do this" (instead of I can't)

"If I don't do this now it will be long" (instead of saying it's long)

"Waking up early *can sometimes* be challenging" (I hate waking up in the morning)

"I have never tried it before but I'm willing to give it a go" (Why try when I will only fail). We underestimate the power of words, sound and the power associated with various combinations of words that form a sentence.

A sentence is a combination of words that create a message. I could be here for a while breaking down the English language but right now, I am committed to ensuring that you understand the importance of why you need to speak to positively to yourself.

What does the word sentence mean to you? According to the English dictionary, the word SENTENCE has two meanings, so let's explore it.

Meaning One

A **sentence** is a linguistic unit consisting of one or more words that are grammatically linked. A sentence can include words grouped meaningfully to express a statement, question, exclamation, request, command or suggestion.

Some sentences can be liberating, creative, magical and life giving when expressed.

Meaning Two

The punishment given to a defendant found guilty by a court,

"Your brother is **serving** a five-year **sentence** for possessing a knife."

Therefore it is VITALLY IMPORTANT that you ensure the SENTENCES that you speak don't sentence your potential and possibilities to a LIFETIME behind bars.

DO NOT SENTENCE YOUR POTENTIAL TO A LIFETIME BEHIND BARS by the sentences you use.

How do you 'use' your sentences? Imagine your words, sentences and tone of voice had magic abilities. Imagine that, your words could sentence someone to lifetime in prison or they could enrich, bless and empower someone's very existence. Imagine a child whose parent tells them every day that they are stupid and ugly. The words of the parent, and the tones used at the time can indeed imprison the child…mentally.

Over time, there have been amazing people who understood the power of their sentences and they were never apologetic for the impact this power had on the world.

The first person I would like to acknowledge is **Robert Nesta "Bob" Marley** who was a Jamaican reggae musician singer-songwriter, who achieved international fame and acclaim. Through his music, Bob Marley shared his worldviews and often celebrated his inspiration, who was Jamaican, Marcus Mosiah Garvey, whose philosophy deeply influenced Bob's song writing.

Many of his songs had anti-imperialist and pro-African themes such as *Zimbabwe, Exodus, Survival*, *Black Man Redemption,* and *Redemption Song.* Interestingly, *Redemption Song* draws influence from a speech given by Marcus Garvey in Nova Scotia, 1937. In the song *Africa Unite,* Bob Marley sings of a desire for all peoples of the African diaspora to come together and fight against '*Babylon*', which represents imperialist and colonialist ideals that have oppressed African people through the eradication of their original culture and beliefs.

Marley believed that the freedom and independence of African countries (such as Zimbabwe) from European domination was a victory for all peoples of the African diaspora.

Bob Marley knew of the power of words and used his power to influence BILLIONS of people.

Lauryn Hill, an American singer–songwriter, rapper, producer, and actress is another artist who understands the power of words. She is best known for being a member of The Fugees and for her solo album, *The Miseducation of Lauryn Hill.* She shared similar views to Bob Marley and these views underpin everything written within No Enemy Within. Take a moment to check out some of her songs particularly *Freedom Time,* taken from the *MTV Unplugged* album.

When I first heard Lauryn Hill recite this song in spoken word on stage I nearly cried. Her voice was so powerful; her words cut through my soul like a hot knife through butter.

NO ENEMY WITHIN

This musical masterpiece is called 'REBEL':

I find it hard to say, that everything is alright
Don't look at me that way, like everything is all right
Cuz my own eyes can see, through all your false pretenses
But what you fail to see, is all the consequences
You think our lives are cheap, and easy to be wasted
As history repeats, so foul you can taste it
And while the people sleep, too comfortable to face it
His life so incomplete and nothing can replace it
And while the people sleep, too comfortable to face it
Your lives so incomplete and nothing can replace it
Fret not thyself I say, against these laws of man
Cuz like the Bible says, His blood is on their hands
And what I gotta say, and what I gotta say, is rebel
While today is still today, choose well
And what I gotta say, is rebel, it can't go down this way
Choose well, choose well, choose well...
...choose well, choose well, and choose well
And while the people sleep, too comfortable to face it
Your lives are so incomplete, and nothing, and no one, can
replace it

No, no, no, no, no, no, no, no, no, no, no, no
And what I gotta say, and what I gotta say
And what I gotta say, and what I gotta say
Is rebel... rebel, rebel, rebel, rebel, rebel, rebel

DAVIS J. WILLIAMS

NO ENEMY WITHIN

Repent, the day is far too spent, rebel... rebel!
Wake up, wake up, wake up, wake up, wake up, wake up,
wake up...
Wake up and rebel
We must destroy in order to rebuild
Wake up, you might as well
Oh are you... oh are you satisfied
Oh are you satisfied
Rebel... ohhh rebel
Why don't you rebel, why don't you rebel?

Why don't you rebel?

Watch your thoughts, they become words.
Watch your words, they become deeds.
Watch your deeds, they become habits.
Watch your habits, they become character.
Character is everything.

DAY 13 CHALLENGE

As Soon As You Wake Up	Focus on what you would like to achieve for the day. Then find a Mirror And READ your PROMISE LETTER. Refer to your BRAND and remind yourself how you need to act
Today's mind-set Challenge	*"What I hear, I forget; What I see, I remember; What I do, I understand."* Research says that you retain 10% of knowledge that you read, 30% of what you see, 50% of what you see and hear, 70% of what you write and say and 90% of what you SAY AND DO. Today you will encourage a small group (more than 2 people) of young people (or anyone you can find) to also be the best they can be. All of the stories you have read should have armed you with a good insight into the benefits of BEING THE BEST YOU CAN BE. TODAY, you are feeling AMAZING and POWERFUL and sharing this knowledge with others will help you retain this way of being. Find a group and MOTIVATE them, INSPIRE them and ENROL them into the possibility that they can be better. Many people FEAR PUBLIC SPEAKING. TODAY YOU WILL EMBRACE THE FEAR!
Before You Go Sleep	Complete your journal and get ready to dominate tomorrow. Do 40 press ups or squats. Create a voice note or video message of your experience so far. HOUR MEDITATION,

JOURNAL ENTRY

HOW WAS DAY 13?

Describe your day. What do you need to improve on? What went well? What did you learn? Write as much as possible!

WELCOME TO **DAY 14**

"You have to believe in yourself when no one else does..."
– SERENA WILLIAMS, TENNIS CHAMPION

"Go on, tell me that I am not good enough, tell me that I can't do it because I will keep on showing you over and over

again that I can" **Davis J Williams**

DAVIS J. WILLIAMS

NO ENEMY WITHIN

Mind Games

By Davis J. Williams

Davis why did you punch him in the face?
It wasn't me, it was my ego

Davis why did you scream and shout over that small incident?
It wasn't me, it was my ego

Davis why did you just embarrass me in front of everyone in class?
It wasn't me, it was my ego

Have you ever caught yourself acting in a way that made you cringe?

I have!

So many times, and my closest and dearest frequently tell me that it is because of my massive ego.

My ego, that slippery snake can be tricky to manage and it has been at the centre of ALL of my trials and tribulations to date!
Just like the time I used to work for Marks and Spencer's, it was a quiet Tuesday evening and I was innocently stacking shelves. Now understand this, I loved working for Marks and Spencer's, the pay was decent, the environment was appealing and I was stress free. Everything was cool until I heard that voice...

'Go to the till and steal some money, go on, don't be a bit*h, you can buy a nice jeans with that"

At first I ignored it, until 5 minutes later that voice returned

"Davis, what you waiting for, go get that money, go get that money, go get that money, go on, what you waiting for? "

The voice wouldn't stop until I decided to listen. I couldn't resist. 25 minutes later I stole £210 from the cashiers till. I was scared at first until the voice reassured me that everything would be ok.

"Davis you're so smart, so slick, you are just awesome, well done, trust me, everything will be ok!"

And the voice was right, everything was ok; no one suspected anything, so my trust in the voice grew. The following week, same time and place the voice returned. However this time it wasn't a pair of jeans that I found myself wanting, it was a laptop and this time the voice was even louder than before.

"Davis, they can't stop you, you are above them, you are so cool, slick and important, take as much money as possible, go on, do it, do it now"

After four months of non-stop stealing I had accumulated over £80,000 worth of card details and products. I eventually got caught, the police got involved and the lesson was learnt.

What was that lesson?

THE EGO, that stupid little voice, is not MY FRIEND and doesn't really care about me.

The EGO was born the same day as me and is just like my shadow; shadows are neither good nor bad. You, me and everyone else has something in us called the ego that diverts us from the true and authentic self that lies within. I once thought that little voice in my head was the real me but I later found that was not the case.

The ego was my first defense mechanism. When I was born my first priority was survival and being new to this overwhelming world I had to create a mask, that mask being my ego. My ego is a false reality I created for the sake of survival.

NO ENEMY WITHIN

The ego is my understanding of myself, the idea I have about who I am, which is actually based on a lie.

If you wear a mask long enough, you begin to forget who you are underneath.

We all wear masks, but just like we all have different fingerprints, our egos are varied.

We easily confuse that little voice in our head with our true 'self' and the ego's constant commentary makes it very difficult to separate the real me from the inauthentic one.

I had to learn how to control my ego; that was my first step to self-awareness; I had to become aware of when my ego tried to take over so I could stop it before disaster happened.

I first became aware of how dangerous and powerful my ego was during my first DetoxHD. My ego went crazy when I first committed to unplugging from social media. It was fighting for its survival, to be heard, to be appreciated, to be obeyed; it would try anything to sabotage my development and begged me to feed it, boy did it try to get me to do some crazy things.

During the DetoxHD the ego revealed itself as my worst enemy. All my other enemies I could avoid and defeat but this enemy was different, it was a part of me.

Here are a few things that I discovered about myself:

1) I thought I had all the answers and no one could tell me anything, even when I was wrong, I was right. My ego always wanted to be right!

2) I always refused the advice of others; my ego hated being told to do anything. I hated authority, I hated advice and I hated anyone who had one up on me, even if it was for my benefit.

3) I would sometimes act superior, as if others were beneath me. I was the boss and the way I would speak to some people was criminal. I always wanted to be right and sometimes I would let people mess up, even if I could have helped, but wouldn't, until they directly came to me.

4) I loved saying "I told you so, you should have listened to me."

5) I thought that people were always out to get me and would be very defensive and paranoid and as a result I wouldn't let anyone get too close. I refused to apologise, even when I was wrong and above all, I loved manipulating and controlling others.

The intention of this short essay is to inspire you, to realise that you are not your thoughts; you are the awareness behind those thoughts. The day you control your ego is the day your life becomes limitless. It is truly time for you to release that inner giant and grasp that dream with both hands. The days of chasing your dreams are over, wake up and catch it.

The ego will be your greatest opponent. I challenge you to take on the ego by embracing that fear and step outside of your comfort zone.

The magic always happens at the end of one's comfort zone.

Can you hear your ego squirm at the thought of you confronting that fear? It's time to step up.

If you are scared of speaking in public it's time to book your first speaking engagement. Are you afraid of heights? Go skydiving. Whatever it is you fear, it's time to silence the ego and overcome.

An old Cherokee told his grandson,

"My son, there is a mighty battle between two wolves inside us all. One is Evil. It is anger, jealousy, greed, resentment, inferiority, lies; it's called the ego. The other is Good. It is joy, peace, love, hope, humility, kindness, empathy and truth. It's called your spirit."

The boy thought about it and asked,

"Grandfather, which wolf wins?"

The old man quietly replied,

"The one you feed"

DAY 14 CHALLENGE

As Soon As You Wake Up	As soon as you wake up focus on what you'd like to achieve for the day. Then find a mirror and READ your PROMISE LETTER - by now you should know it by heart!
Today's Mind-set Challenge	**'Bang Bang Your Dead' -** You're at a **funeral**. It's your turn to read a speech about the person who died. That person who died is **you**, the OLD you, not the **new and amazing** you but the person who held you back and stopped you from achieving greatness. Write your eulogy **on a minimum of one side of A4** and say bye to the old **YOU. SAY GOODBYE THEN PHYSCIALLY BURN IT IN FRONT OF YOUR INNER CIRCLE. Perform a ritual WHERE you say good bye to the old self - THEN CELEBRATE!!!!!!!!**
Before You Go Sleep	Complete your journal and get ready to dominate tomorrow. Do 40 press ups or squats. Create a voice note or video message of your experience so far.

JOURNAL ENTRY

HOW WAS DAY 14?

Describe your day. What do you need to improve on? What went well? What did you learn? Write as much as possible!

Bonus Story by Peaches Cadogan

From the beginning I always had a problem with confronting/challenging myself and being face to face with my internal conflict and people's opinions of me. This fight with people's distorted truths and warped sense of reality was constant; one day I decided I really wanted to break the vicious cycle that had impacted and contaminated my family and prevented us from progressing in life with unity and love. There seemed to be a real lack of self-love and love of family.

Everyone has their own truth, whether it is fighting demons or dancing with angels. That raw honest awareness of decisions and perception of the world is one that cannot be ignored and the starting point of healing.

For years I have listened to people deny truths, and secrets being down played a vital part in personal development but due to bad habits and contradictory language being used on a daily have had a huge contribution of holding prisoners mentally, emotionally, spiritually and physically.

Now it is that time to make the right choices, decisions for self, take responsibility of your own growth and grow. It is vital to know your purpose. Why it is important to break that vicious cycle? Could it be because it has a negative impact on your life and that of your loved ones? Ask yourself honestly, what are the benefits of making the right decisions for you? Knowing the reason why will bring things back into perspective and motivate you to embrace you and truly live. Live with love and integrity because you love and know thyself, manage yourself well and manage every aspect of your life with TRUTH and conviction.

CONGRATULATIONS – YOU MADE IT

Well done, and congratulations! You have completed the detox HD. How did you do?

How did you find the whole experience? Please share your thoughts!

Now that you have finished your DetoxHD you have to start using all the tasks you used during the past 14 days in your life.

Be the better version of yourself.

WARNING: Do not let this be your last DetoxHD - Join in on the next one and take your vision and potential to the next level.

Imagine if your whole team to committed to this DetoxHD how productive things would be.

The people you surround yourself with will ultimately lift you higher.

Connect with the squad - share your story

No Enemy Within

How to build a legendary character aims to help you become the best possible version of yourself and we believe that by completing this 14-day mindset boot camp you will meet the person who you always wanted to be.

Just like this book helped TRANSFORM you, now it's your turn help transform someone else.

Share your story, your experience, a story, an essay, a challenge and be responsible for someone else's transformation

Submit your contributions to hello@davisjwilliams.com for a chance to feature in NO ENEMY WITHIN <u>VOLUME 2</u>

FINAL THOUGHT

PLEASE COMPLETE THIS FINAL TASK

CREATE A BETTER POSSIBILITY FOR YOURSELF

Now that I have finished this detoxHD I will now………..

Biographies & Contributions

This book would not have been possible if these amazingly talented
If their story inspired you please connect with them.

Leah Salmon
http://thenaturallyyoucoach.com/

Michelle Thorney
http://www.beyoutifulbeginnings.org.uk/

Julian Hall
http://www.julianhall.co.uk/

Kandice Bryan
https://www.facebook.com/kandice.bryan?fref=ts

Warren Ryan
https://www.linkedin.com/pub/warren-ryan/43/645/188

Andrew Muhammad
http://theinvestigator.org.uk/

Swiss (So Solid Crew)
http://www.theguardian.com/music/2005/apr/24/urban

Peaches Cadogan
https://uk.linkedin.com/in/peachesrealitybytesuk

Special thank you goes out to you!
Our network DETERMINES our net – **WORTH**

Davis J Williams:
Teaches children to play chess / Once stopped a stabbing and risked his life / Acted as a consultant to addressing gangs for the government on more than one occasion / Has the ability to be several places at once / Hand-delivered food, toys and medical supplies to villages in Gambia / Worked in prisons across the UK inspiring others / Cycled 60 miles raising money for a Sickle Cell charity / Helped thousands of students get into college and university / Helped raise money and build a playground for victims of a tsunami / Helped countless of young people exit local 'gangs' / Survived a shooting by dodging the bullets / Found homes for the homeless / helped secure thousands of pounds for a local inner city charity / A raw food chef and advisor / Fitness Instructor / Once saved a cat from a tree / An active father / Multi – entrepreneur / Motivational speaker / Juggling four jobs and finds time to watch Arsenal play / Wrote an amazing book teaching others to do the same…or even better.

www.davisjwilliams.com

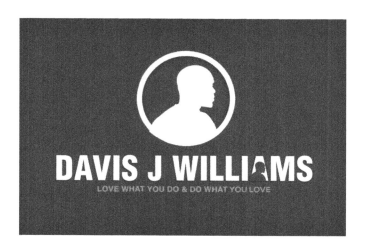